Routledge Revivals

Heredity and Child Culture

Heredity and Child Culture

Henry Dwight Chapin

First published in 1923 by George Routledge & Sons Ltd.

This edition first published in 2018 by Routledge
2 Park Square, Milton Park, Abingdon, Oxon, OX14 4RN
and by Routledge
711 Third Avenue, New York, NY 10017

Routledge is an imprint of the Taylor & Francis Group, an informa business

© 1923 by Taylor & Francis

All rights reserved. No part of this book may be reprinted or reproduced or utilised in any form or by any electronic, mechanical, or other means, now known or hereafter invented, including photocopying and recording, or in any information storage or retrieval system, without permission in writing from the publishers.

Publisher's Note
The publisher has gone to great lengths to ensure the quality of this reprint but points out that some imperfections in the original copies may be apparent.

Disclaimer
The publisher has made every effort to trace copyright holders and welcomes correspondence from those they have been unable to contact.

A Library of Congress record exists under ISBN: 22018296

ISBN 13: 978-1-138-61670-7 (hbk)
ISBN 13: 978-0-429-46187-3 (ebk)

COMPOSITE FIGURE SHOWING COMPLETELY DEVELOPED YOUTH.

Heredity and Child Culture

BY

HENRY DWIGHT CHAPIN, M.D.

*President of the Children's Welfare Federation of New York;
Medical Director of the Speedwell Society; Emeritus Professor of Medicine (Diseases of Children) at the
New York Post-Graduate Medical School
and Hospital; Ex-President of
the American Pediatric
Society*

WITH A FOREWORD BY

PROFESSOR HENRY FAIRFIELD OSBORN

WITH A FRONTISPIECE

LONDON
GEORGE ROUTLEDGE & SONS, LIMITED
BROADWAY HOUSE: 68-74 Carter Lane
1923

TO

MY FRIEND AND CLASS-MATE

HENRY FAIRFIELD OSBORN

Preface

In a study of the developmental period, one must start with a background relating to influences that precede the beginning of independent life and which tend to give it a good or bad start. With this in mind, I have briefly sketched the views of some leading biologists on the subject of heredity, and have freely drawn upon various authorities who have written on the subjects discussed. Their names, with references, are mentioned in the text, and I herewith express my obligation to them.

As to the factors that control life after it has begun, those occurring in the early years are the ones that specially count. Hence this period of life must be particularly stressed in a study of the possibilities of development. It is also well to know what to expect when conditions are favourable and how to recognize disastrous influences in time for correction. This involves a study of the various problems of children as individuals as well as in their social relationships.

Good development is the resultant of many forces, among which may be noted heredity, prenatal care of the expectant mother, proper oversight of infants and growing children, food, iv

PREFACE

clothing, housing, education, hours and conditions of study, recreation, expert medical attendance during illness, and the general habits of the individual.

In the frontispiece is shown a statue representing the physical perfection of form in youth. The sculptor is Professor R. Tait McKensie of the University of Pennsylvania, and the figure stands in the American Museum of Natural History. In proportions it represents an average of the fifty strongest men at Harvard as measured by Dr. Dudley A. Sargent. I am indebted to Professor McKensie for photographing the figure for me and permitting its use in this book.

HENRY DWIGHT CHAPIN.

Contents

CHAPTER		PAGE
I.	IMPORTANCE OF THE CHILD	3
II.	ORGANIC INHERITANCE	10
III.	SOCIAL INHERITANCE	20
IV.	SELECTIVE BREEDING	32
V.	THE BEGINNING OF LIFE	43
VI.	THE DEVELOPING PERIOD	52
VII.	THE PRE-SCHOOL AGE	66
VIII.	THE SCHOOL CHILD	73
IX.	MENTAL CULTURE	96
X.	MORAL CULTURE	109
XI.	NERVE CULTURE	119
XII.	THE IMPORTANCE OF PROPER NUTRITION	124
XIII.	THE FAMILY	140
XIV.	THE DEPENDENT CHILD	149
XV.	THE ADOPTION OF CHILDREN	172
XVI.	THE PROLONGATION OF HUMAN LIFE THROUGH CHILD CULTURE	185

Foreword

IT is very important that all parents, all teachers, and all physicians should understand the interlocking relations of heredity and environment. So much reliance is placed on education in America that it is necessary to stress the great importance of being born with a sound and healthy constitution and with good moral, spiritual, and intellectual predispositions.

Heredity is, in fact, altogether a matter of predisposition and potentiality; it is the key which fits the lock of environment, including all the steps in nurture and in education. Consequently, eugenics, which has to do with being born well, and euthenics, which has to do with being nurtured and educated well, have been inseparable from the beginning of time.

The value of a clear understanding of these principles to the parent, teacher and physician, begins with birth and extends through the entire life education, when the responsibility of the world's welfare passes on to another generation. If there is an hereditary predisposition, —a passion for drink, for instance,—and we know of it, we can, through nurture and environment, take away the opportunity for its development; if there is an hereditary predisposition to certain physical defects, such as tuberculosis,

vii

FOREWORD

we can, by change of environment and proper nurture prevent its development.

During the last seventy-five years we have made marvellous progress in euthenics, and I believe we are on the threshold of similar progress in eugenics. The two fields of humanitarian endeavour interlock exactly as heredity interlocks with environment, nature with nurture.

The writer of this volume is one of the leaders of our time in the application of knowledge inspired by sentiment and real sympathy and understanding of the ills to which flesh is heir. In this work we find clearly set forth this most important of all humanitarian movements, namely, the birth and care of children.

The nation that takes the best care of the birth of its children, that encourages the kinds of birth which will bring into the world the greatest amount of happiness and the least amount of suffering, and the nation that brings to the care of children after birth all the advantages of education in its broadest sense, is destined to survive and lead the world in the progress of the future.

Let us pray that this may be our American nation.

HENRY FAIRFIELD OSBORN.

HEREDITY AND CHILD CULTURE

" *The children must be practised well to this, or they'll ne'er do't.*"

" *I will teach the children their behaviours.*"
—SHAKESPEARE, The Merry Wives of Windsor.

" *The Youth of a Nation are the Trustees of Posterity.*"
—DISRAELI.

" *And a little child shall lead them.*"—ISAIAH, xi, 6.

Heredity and Child Culture

CHAPTER I

IMPORTANCE OF THE CHILD

Two controlling factors are present in all life,—heredity and environment, nature and nurture, as expressed by Galton. At the birth of the individual, heredity has done its best or its worst, and can be reckoned with only in the sense of having all the best potentialities and predispositions cherished and developed, and all the worst avoided. Its activity has extended through long or short reaches of past time, and the laws of its operation are not completely understood. The question of environment and nurture being of the present, and to a certain extent possible of control, now assumes the greatest importance. While from the biologic standpoint heredity may appear to be the more important influence, yet in the scheme of evolution the higher the animal the more important and influential become nurture and environment. This is especially emphasized in the human race by the prolongation of the

4 HEREDITY AND CHILD CULTURE

period of infancy. John Fiske was the first to elaborate this fruitful view of one of the fundamental laws of higher evolution, that not only throws a strong light on the methods of evolution but lays the greatest importance upon the period of infancy as influencing the future development and usefulness of the individual.

This long period of helpless infancy is a time of extreme plasticity when the career of the individual is no longer predetermined by the career of its ancestor. One generation of the lower animals is nearly an exact reproduction of the preceding one. The young animal is born almost fully formed and can look out for itself at once or shortly after birth, independently of the parent. The longer the infancy and growing time of an animal the longer the period of its teachability; and a slow growth means an increase both in capacity for development and of all the loftier prerogatives. Thus the higher apes have a babyhood when for two or three months they are unable to feed themselves or move about independently of the parent. The human infant is distinguished from the highest of the lower animals by the much longer duration of helpless infancy and the marked increase in the size of the brain, particularly in the extent of its surface. There is

IMPORTANCE OF THE CHILD 5

here a great increase in the size and complexity of brain organization that takes place largely after birth. Accompanying the rapid growth of the nervous system is that of the skeleton and various visceral organs.

During the first two years of life, the brain not only doubles in weight but increases marvelously in its convolutions and complexity. The infinite distance between man and the lower animals consists in the fact that, in the former, natural selection confines itself principally to the surface of the brain, which requires a long period of helpless infancy for this highly plastic work to be properly started and developed. Inherited tendencies are there, but the proper environment counts for much in this work, so potent in future possibilities.

It is evident that, correlated with this long period of infancy there must be a time of maternal care and watchfulness if the race is to exist in health and vigour. Knowledge is required as well as care, for mistakes made at this time can never be completely corrected. The first few years of life are, biologically speaking, the most important ones we live. The beginning organism has at this time stamped on it the possibilities of future vigorous life or of early degeneration and decay. This is

6   HEREDITY AND CHILD CULTURE

to a certain extent true all through the period of childhood, from birth to adolescence. Hence a careful study and understanding of all the phases of infancy and childhood are of the greatest importance alike to physicians, parents and society at large. This is the only period where really constructive and permanent work can be accomplished. Through intelligent direction children may be taken out of environments which will develop the worst and placed in surroundings that will nurture the best.

There has probably been no era in the history of the world when such importance must be attached to the coming generation. Sir George Newman,[1] in a report on the health of English school-children, well states that the War, more than anything else, has brought home to the public the conception of the child as a primary national asset, and that no investment and no national economy can compare in results with the care of the rising generation.

Civilization itself seems to be at the parting of the ways. All kinds of wild and destructive theories are in the air. It is certain that radical and abrupt changes, which are manifestations of primitive intellectual and emotional reactions, will result in disaster. These elemen-

[1] *British Medical Journal*, Oct. 6th, 1917.

IMPORTANCE OF THE CHILD 7

tal passions and strivings that find outlet in lawlessness and revolt are a result of an intellectual and emotional instability that are reversions to the childhood of the race. It has been well said that we have had a world in conflict ; now we have a world in revolt. We are living in an unstable, shell-shocked age.

It is only by starting with the child and building up a sound physical, mental and moral structure that the future manhood can carry on successfully and erect a safer social structure. To prepare a better world, we must provide better men and women, physically, mentally and morally,—and we should start with the child. Broken physiques, like old sinners, are hard to help or control. Many biologists believe that the human race is degenerating and losing some of its old stamina.

The call of the day is for conservation,—of effort, of food, of health, and, above all, of life itself. But merely saving life is not enough. It should be rendered strong and efficient. We have recently had warnings that we must improve our methods in handling the mental and physical life of the time. A high percentage of rejections for physical reasons among the young men of the country, drawn by draft or volunteering in the army,—averaging one in four,—

8   HEREDITY AND CHILD CULTURE

gives food for thought. There must be a sustained and prolonged effort all along the line for improving these conditions.

What is the way out? Many foolish and inadequate theories are advanced, but eventually it must come through the child. The present nerve-shattered generation must get along as best it may, but we must start at the foundations and build a better, stronger race for the future. We can try and beget a sounder generation and so train it as to secure strong bodies, steady nerves, broad judgment and wide vision. We can only avoid a threatened racial impoverishment through the child. Not only is the physical development supremely important in the opening years, but mental and moral impressions experienced during this period, although often forgotten, may deeply affect later life.

The future of the world depends on the child. All advance, all the new orientation the world has hoped for and largely failed in attaining, may come in the new generation if the children can only be properly moulded. All the unsolved individual and social problems may be more hopefully approached if we can but prepare better material with which to make the effort.

IMPORTANCE OF THE CHILD 9

What can we do about heredity? How can environment be best controlled? How can we secure a better race?

Upon the proper answer to these questions depends the future of civilization. The first and sure thing to do is this,—CONCENTRATE ON THE CHILD.

CHAPTER II

ORGANIC INHERITANCE

THE writer is not a pure scientist but a practical worker who has devoted many years to a study of the actual problems of childhood. Some of the apparent laws of biology, as promulgated by various interpreters, seem to point to a sort of hopeless determinism. An effort is here made to glance at these laws from a different angle, to see if a more encouraging outlook cannot be maintained.

Which is the preponderating and all-important influence in life, nature or nurture, heredity or environment? Both are vitally important, but which must be stressed in our thought and action? Upon the answer to this question depends much of our attitude toward some of the pressing problems of life. If the first is over-emphasized, we shall, at best, be landed in a sort of benevolent fatalism; if the second looms up in importance, it encourages hope and effort. This question starts with the beginning of life and ends with its close.

ORGANIC INHERITANCE 11

It is at the beginning, however, that it assumes the greatest importance for here is where change and accomplishment are possible.

The evolution of all life, plant as well as animal, depends upon the action of the following great forces,—heredity, reproduction, variation and environment. Let us glance at some of the ideas held by various biologists on the subject of heredity. The older views were advanced by Lamarck and Darwin. Lamarck believed that organisms could be modified by environment, and such modifications occurring during the life of the animal could be passed along by organic inheritance. This view, of course, stressed the influence of environment and held that evolution proceeds by means of the inheritance of acquired characters. These characters that might proceed from use, need or desire, formed the basis of progressive evolution. He stated that "all that has been acquired or altered in the organization of individuals during their lives is preserved by generation and transmitted by individuals who sprang from those who have undergone these changes." By developing functional activity of organs, in other words, by constantly employing them, hereditary as well as other

12   HEREDITY AND CHILD CULTURE

values could be obtained.   Thus developed the idea known as *use inheritance.*

Darwin believed that evolution takes place through natural selection or the struggle for existence and the survival of the fittest.   This, as well as other forms of variability, may depend on changing conditions of life.   He held that alterations in the environment acting directly or indirectly on the animal might produce variation in inheritance by becoming cumulative through a series of generations.   Conversely, individuals, families and races that can not adapt themselves to a changing environment will gradually yield to the law of natural selection and disappear.   Families and races that fail to properly reproduce will yield more quickly to this law both as to cause and effect. These opinions are becoming displaced in the minds of many biologists by what may be considered a more modern view.

Independent life begins by the union of two cells, the ovum and sperm cell, which is known as *conception.*   The influences of heredity are then closed as far as this individual life is concerned and any further influence upon development must come from environment.   It has been well said that after conception the mother is only a nurse to the child.   The modern biol-

ORGANIC INHERITANCE 13

ogist, however, lays the greatest stress upon the nature and influence of these germinal cells. This germinal substance, minute as it is, as distinguished from the rest of the body, is entirely distinct, and little, if at all, influenced by the other tissues. A radical distinction is thus drawn between the germ and the *soma*, as the rest of the body is called. The only characteristics that can be passed along by organic inheritance are such as have been contained in the germinal substance of the egg and the sperm cell. The direct implication from this doctrine is that the condition of the body as a whole, apart from the germ cells, has no influence upon inheritance. This naturally leads up to the doctrine of Weismann that acquired characters are not transmitted by inheritance. While traits may be transmitted that the individual has himself inherited, those that have been acquired by his own actions cannot be passed on to posterity. This germ plasm continues along through different generations as an unending stream and each individual body acts as a receptacle and conserver of an imperishable part.

The most vital part of every body cell is a minute spot called *the nucleus*. In the sex cells there are located in the nuclei marvellously

14 HEREDITY AND CHILD CULTURE

minute germinal units known as *chromosomes.*
Each of these chromosomes contains deter-
miners, every one of which acts as a determin-
ant of some hereditary character.   It is even
believed that a special spot in each chromosome
holds the determiner for each character.   Different chromosomes may come from different
ancestors and they may be combined in many
varying ways, which accounts for different
traits seen in the offspring. As there are
numerous possible and diverse combinations of
these ancestral germ units, we can understand
how varying may be the characteristics of
different individuals.   Numberless combinations may be possible as it has been estimated
that there are 48 chromosomes in the sex cells
of the white woman.   It is further supposed
that variation may be caused by a recombi-
nation of these ancestral germ units in future
generations, as well as by changes that may
take place in the germ plasm itself.   Prolonged undernourishment and various poisons
may ultimately have a disastrous effect upon
the germ plasm.   It is not supposed, however,
that changes in the body plasm or soma can
have direct effect on the germ plasm.

One of the most interesting theories concern-
ing the method of action of heredity is known

ORGANIC INHERITANCE 15

as Mendelism, a term taken from the name of Gregor Mendel by whom it was first elaborated. According to this theory, the unit characters in the sex cells do not blend but remain distinct and are thus passed along at birth. These characters always retain their individuality, and when they are different and exclusive, the more active character is said to be dominant and the more passive one recessive. Mendel believed that paired characters received from the parents are so segregated in the ovum and sperm cell of the offspring that only one of the characters is contained in each of these germ cells. Thus when there are two contrasted pairs of characters in the parent only one (dominant) will appear in the offspring. These distinct characters are called pure, and the essential fact of Mendel's law is that the characters in the germ cells always retain their purity or distinctiveness. In the offspring of hybrids 25 per cent. of dominant and recessive characters will reappear as pure. It is generally found that the characters, dominant and recessive, transmitted by hybrids will be split in a general ratio of three to one.

Professor Edwin Grant Conklin[1] defines

---

[1] *Heredity and Environment in the Development of Men.*—Princeton University Press,

16 HEREDITY AND CHILD CULTURE

heredity as the particular germinal organization that is transmitted from parents to offspring. To quote,—" Heritage is the sum of all those qualities which are determined or caused by this germinal organization. Development is progressive and co-ordinated differentiation of this germinal organization by which it is transferred into the adult organization." Again, " Inherited traits are not transmitted from parents to offspring but the germinal factors or causes are transmitted, and under proper conditions of environment these give rise to developed characters. Every oosperm as well as every developed organism differs more or less from every other one, and this remarkable condition is brought about by extremely numerous permutations in the distribution of the chromosomes of the sex cells in maturation and fertilization." Professor Henry Fairfield Osborn, in his remarkable book. *The Origin and Evolution of Life*, falls back on an energy conception of life. Some of his ideas are put in a striking way as follows,—" We know to some extent *how* plants and animals evolve ; we do not know *why* they evolve * * * * * All the explanations of evolution which have been offered by three generations of naturalists align themselves under two main ideas only. The

ORGANIC INHERITANCE 17

first is the idea that the causes of evolution are chiefly from without inward, namely, beginning in the environment of the body and extending into the germ ; this idea is *centripetal.* The second idea is just the reverse : it is *centrifugal*, namely, that the causes begin in the germ and extend outward and into the body and into the environment. * * * * * Weismann's great contribution to thought has been to point out the very sharp distinction which undoubtedly exists between the hereditary forces and predispositions in the heredity-germ and the visable expression of these forces in the organism. The problem of causes of evolution has become an infinitely more difficult one since Weismann has compelled us to realize that the essential question is the *causes of germinal evolution* rather than the causes of bodily evolution or of environmental evolution. * * * * * The idea that the germ is an energy complex is an as yet unproved hypothesis ; it has not been demonstrated. The heredity-germ in some respects bears a likeness to latent or potential interacting energy, while in other respects it is entirely unique. The supposed germ energy is not only cumulative but is in a sense imperishable, self-perpetuating,

B

18 HEREDITY AND CHILD CULTURE

and continuous during the whole period of the evolution of life upon the earth. * * * * * While we owe to matter and form the revelation of the existence of the great *law* of evolution, we must reserve our thought in the search for causes and take steps toward an energy conception of the origin of life and an energy conception of the nature of heredity."

Although the theories of hereditary action are thus somewhat diverse, certain general facts may be noted upon which there is agreement. Herbert Spencer defines heredity as the law that each plant or animal, if it reproduces, gives origin to others like itself, the likeness consisting not so much in the repetition of individual traits as in the assumption of the same general structure.

According to Galton's law of ancestral inheritance, the two parents contribute between them on an average one-half of each inherited quality, one-fourth being contributed by each of them. The four grandparents contribute one-sixteenth, or altogether one-fourth of the inherited faculties, and the further back one goes the less will naturally be the influence. Pearson, another authority, believes that parents have relatively more influence than grandparents, as indicated in the above ratio,

ORGANIC INHERITANCE 19

although accepting the general principle of the law of ancestral inheritance.

It must be acknowledged that in respect to organic heredity there are many gaps in our knowledge, and it must also be borne in mind that most of the studies of biologists have been made upon plants and the lower animals and their generalizations can only partly apply to human beings. In the scheme of evolution, the higher the animal the slower and more important becomes its period of growth. This is especially emphasized, as already noted, in human beings by the prolongation of the period of infancy and the many subsequent years of growth before complete development is obtained. It accordingly follows that heredity seems to be more important as an influence in the lower organisms than in man.

CHAPTER III

SOCIAL INHERITANCE

In a recent valuable discussion on the question of social heredity and evolution, Professor Herbert William Conn [1] has plainly shown how the laws of the evolution of animals and plants apply to human evolution only up to a certain point, beyond which man has been under the influence of distinct laws of his own. He draws attention to facts proving that the human social unit has been developed by a new set of forces which have had little or no influence in the animal kingdom. Moreover, these forces are under the control, to some extent, of society and the individual.

In line with this thought, Professor E. G. Conklin states that a relatively poor inheritance with excellent environmental conditions often produces better results than a good inheritance with poor conditions. He further believes that hereditary possibilities may remain latent and

[1] *Social Heredity and Social Evolution: The Other Side of Eugenics —* The Abington Press.

SOCIAL INHERITANCE 21

undeveloped unless stimulated into activity by environment.

This leads to the distinction that may be made between individual and social evolution, the forces of which are controlled by different laws. For the individual we have biological heredity; for society we have what may properly be called a social heredity that passes along accumulations gained by parents from the surrounding civilization—in other words, from the environment. These are the acquired characters that can be passed along from parents to offspring by teaching and example, although not by direct biological inheritance. While the latter, according to modern science, cannot be immediately influenced, the social inheritance and evolution of the individual can be powerfully affected by education.

A glance at some of the characters that may be acquired by social heredity shows how large a number of important influences lie entirely outside organic heredity.

What are the principal acquirements that the parent has already learned from his surroundings and can thus teach to his offspring? These have been well summarized by Professor Conn. The first and most fundamental acquirement is language. This is evidently a

22 HEREDITY AND CHILD CULTURE

social inheritance as the infant of the most cultured parents is just as unable to speak as the offspring of mentally deficient people. While a few of the lower animals emit sounds that doubtless possess rudimentary efforts towards the exercise of language, the human animal has reached full development in civilization and knowledge through this constantly exercised social inheritance that is at first gained by simple imitation and not by organic inheritance. A new-born baby of the present age is just as helpless as if born in the stone age, and probably essentially the same in organic nature.

Not only the use of spoken words but the ability to write them down is another example of social inheritance that lays the foundation for all knowledge. The possibilities of learning thus come largely through social relationships. The great accumulation of facts and generalizations leading to laws that partially explain many of the phenomena of nature and life could not have been preserved or passed along from generation to generation without the ability to record them and thus elevate and ennoble the mind. Professor Stewart Paton [1] puts it thus—"If we recognize that the mind is largely a social product, we shall avoid many

[1] *Human Behaviour*—Charles Scribner's Sons.

SOCIAL INHERITANCE 23

of the unnecessary difficulties introduced into the discussion of the inheritance of mental characteristics. Because of the fact that the mental make-up is, to a considerable extent the result of environmental stimuli, it is to be considered as a 'social contribution.' Mental potentiality is conditioned by heredity, but development is encouraged or inhibited very largely by what happens after birth. There is also some reason to believe that changes in nurture may serve as stimuli affecting the growth of the embryo through the parental germ cells."

The existence of a moral sense that can distinguish right from wrong is not born with the individual. The infant has no moral sense and is a perfect example of unadulterated selfishness. Conscience, that best trait of later life, does not exist at the start. Altruistic traits that really form the foundation of what is best in modern civilization are not found at the beginning of life but must be cultivated by instruction and example—in other words, they are socially acquired. The possibilities of moral development may doubtless vary according to innate inheritances which are influenced by organic conditions, but the superstructure must be acquired by the teaching and example of others.

24   HEREDITY AND CHILD CULTURE

The very construction and existence of society depend upon numerous and diverse social inheritances. The functioning of government, the accumulation of wealth, many artificial conditions of environment that minister to the higher life of the race, and numerous other factors that distinguish human life from mere animal life proceed from social ideals that are handed on from generation to generation. The origin and continuance of the human family is largely owing to the same influence. It is thus evident that the evolution of the organic body as such and the evolution of society, proceed according to laws that are widely divergent, but the higher traits in human evolution and in civilization itself depend on social, and not on organic, inheritance.

While some lower forms of life, as bees and ants, show organization in a remarkable degree, it is due to instinct that plays only a minor part in human development. Instincts are due entirely to organic inheritance and function owing to a certain definite structure of nerve centres and ganglia. These ganglia always give the same automatic response to all stimuli with changeless uniformity. It is thus the structure of the nervous system that accounts for the wonderful phenomena often

SOCIAL INHERITANCE 25

exhibited by the instincts and these do not depend on learning or experience. While the lower animals are guided by their instincts, man exhibits an initiative power drawn from acquired knowledge.

It is thus seen that a broader view of all the conditions surrounding heredity makes for a more hopeful outlook for human beings as distinguished from lower animals. At first view, Weismann's theory that every child is moulded solely by inherited tendencies that cannot be essentially altered, and that acquired traits are not transmitted, seems to make for a loss of personal responsibility and a pessimistic outlook. Granting that this may be true on the strictly biologic side, we have the possibility of a wide and splendid social inheritance that may do much to shape life's currents and even compensate for some of the defects of organic heritage.

Some of our leading biologists seem to be taking more hopeful views. Professor Doncaster [1] observes that what is inherited is not the character acquired but the innate power of acquiring it. While the germ cell determines whether and to what extent a change shall

[1] *Heredity*—Cambridge University Press.

26   HEREDITY AND CHILD CULTURE

take place, the environment supplies the stimulus.

Professor Conklin states that the experiences and accomplishments of past generations are not inherited through the germ cells but through society.   Then he makes the following trenchant remark,—" Social heredity has out-run germinal heredity and the intellectual, social, and moral responsibilities of our times are too great for many men." This is one of our present-day troubles, as the physical, intellectual and social developments of the age have out-distanced its moral development. Lathrop Stoddart [1] puts it thus,—" The truth is that as civilization advances it leaves behind multitudes of human beings who have not the capacity to keep pace. * * * * * These are not 'degenerates'; they are 'primitives,' carried over into a social environment in which they do not belong." The intelligence tests made upon large numbers of young men recruited for the army during the last war showed an astonishingly large number of morons whose mental age did not exceed twelve years.

Again to quote Professor Conn,—" Our eugenists tell us that an evil trait may persist in a family for generations in spite of any kind

[1] *The Revolt Against Civilization*—Charles Scribner's Sons.

SOCIAL INHERITANCE 27

of training and even in spite of mating with one in whom the weakness is lacking. The laws of organic heredity make it hopeless to strive in any kind of life either to eradicate a weakness or to introduce strength into the nature of our children. Personal responsibility thus tends to vanish entirely as we become filled with this conception. We do not seem responsible for our own acts, inasmuch as they are determined by our inherited traits, 'nor are we responsible for our children's inheritance, since it is beyond our reach. The life one lives seems to weigh as nothing and to be without any influence. * * * * * Among animals, individuals certainly are not responsible either for their own inheritance or that of their offspring. But when we realize that human social evolution has not been an organic one, and that it has been due, not to con-genital but to acquired characters, not to organic but to social heredity, the sense of responsibility for our lives comes back to us with greater force than ever. It is exactly these acquired characters that are forming the future. It is the *lives that men live* that create social inheri-tance. It is not a matter of indifference to our children or to posterity in general what kind of life we individually live. We are responsible for the social heritage that we give our children,

28 HEREDITY AND CHILD CULTURE

even if we are not responsible for their organic heritage. We may greatly modify the social inheritance of our offspring, even after they are born, though we may not modify their organic inheritance; and in determining what they will become and what they will do in the world, the social inheritance commonly counts much more than the organic inheritance. * * * * * The heritage of the race is determined more by what men do than by what they inherit from their parents by organic inheritance. * * * * * Organic heredity simply gives us certain powers, while social heredity determines what we shall do with those powers. Man is moulded into a social individual by social forces, and whether or not he fits into our society depends more upon the social forces at work than upon the powers that nature gave him. Even though he have an inheritance weak both mentally and morally, an individual may be moulded into a fairly good member of the social organism if he is surrounded by proper environment; but if he is reared in the wrong environment, tending to produce a wrong social inheritance, he will be an undesirable member of society, no matter what may have been his innate powers. * * * * * The real stimulus which has acted upon man to produce

SOCIAL INHERITANCE 29

his wonderful development in contrast to animals has been the utilization of the new force of social inheritance."

These hopeful and stimulating words may serve as added warning not to put too much stress upon biological generalizations derived exclusively from plant and animal life. What is often attributed to organic inheritance may, in the last analysis, be largely due to social inheritance. Do the children of thieves, drunkards, and prostitutes turn out badly principally because of birth, or from living in the company and with the example of degenerates? It may be that some individual developments attributed to organic heredity are, to a large extent really due to environment. This thought might be applied to two classic examples in heredity. The children of the Jukes' family, we must remember, were brought up by the Jukes, and the Edwards' family were surrounded by elevating and stimulating influences from birth. Perhaps the Edwards owed about as much to an ideal social as to a good organic heritage.

For many years I was one of the directors of the Children's Village located in the country near New York. Incorrigible boys are committed here by the courts for necessary restraint

30   HEREDITY AND CHILD CULTURE

and education, after committing petty crimes. At the Village they are sent to school in a cottage community, given vocational training, and their energies have free outlet in outdoor sports. In other words, they are given a good social environment to take the place of former bad surroundings. The great majority of these children eventually turn out well. Many have been sent West where they have made good citizens and some have even become eminent in their communities. Doubtless a large number of these unfortunate children started with a fairly good organic inheritance, but, whether they did or not, a bad social inheritance was immediately responsible for their downfall, and, when this was corrected, a favorable result nearly always followed. Many similar endeavours have shown equally good results. Defective eyesight, faulty hearing, diseased tonsils and adenoids, are often causes of poor school records and truancy that may lead to petty crimes.

The following quotation from Ferguson[1] sums up fairly well what many practical workers believe in reference to the factors in human heredity,—" In lower reaches of the process, as compared with the higher, heredity

[1] *The Affirmative Intellect*—Funk & Wagnalls Co.

SOCIAL INHERITANCE 31

is relatively strong. It is likely enough that characteristics acquired in the lifetime of the individual are, in the lower orders, transmitted by heredity, but in higher life this seems generally not to be the case. Heredity is seen to be a failing thing, and the privileges that depend upon it are, with the advancement of the world, ever shorter and shorter lived. The competencies that avail in the highest circles cannot in any considerable measure be passed on from generation to generation, but must be won out of the infinite by each individual for himself. In all that is great and prevailing an organism is born not of the flesh."

There are many with a good biological heredity who have never attained a good social heredity,—in other words, they have never had a fair chance. They form the "mute, inglorious Miltons" in every country churchyard that Gray sang about in his immortal Elegy.

CHAPTER IV

SELECTIVE BREEDING

In stressing the idea that many of our best endowments are conferred by social inheritance, we must remember that these advantages cannot come to their best fruition unless based on a good organic inheritance. The eugenist tells us that the principal method by which racial improvement can take place consists in letting good stock reproduce and poor stock remain sterile. This means that every possible measure should be taken to increase the fertility of the best types. Superior racial stocks must always be encouraged.

A recent article by Major Leonard Darwin, [1] after discussing the danger from propagation of inferior stocks, contains the following statements,—"Turning to the other side of the question, namely the endeavour to increase the fertility of the stocks above the average in racial value and thus to improve the average health

[1] *International Journal of Public Health*, Vol. II, No. 6, 1921.

SELECTIVE BREEDING 33

of future generations, progress in this direction would be promoted by a widespread knowledge of the laws of natural inheritance. Such a knowledge would create a tendency to shun marrying into a family notably inferior in mental or physical qualities, and this tendency ought to be encouraged. . . . Sexual selection has often in nature produced marvellous changes in both the minds and the bodies of animals, and by the aid of conscious efforts sexual selection could be made to produce far more beneficial results to the human race than it is doing at present."

He thus believes that natural heredity can be utilized as an agency for promoting the welfare of mankind. He also calls attention to an endeavour, not dependent on natural inheritance, namely, that of trying to improve the health of our descendants by preventing children from being infected or poisoned before birth by the mothers.

Sir George Newman[1] makes the following observation,—" If we are to grow a sound and healthy race of men we must begin where all true breeding begins, *at the source*. If we

---

[1] *An Outline of the Practice of Preventive Medicine*—Ministry of Health.

C

34 HEREDITY AND CHILD CULTURE

permit ourselves to favour and provide for the unguided propagation of a population of poor physique or of persons marked from birth with the stigmata of alcohol, venereal disease or mental deficiency, we shall sooner or later discover that we are building on false foundations, and without taking sufficiently into our reckoning the laws of heredity, of transmission, and of ante-natal infection."

It does not need a biologist to tell us that reproduction will yield the best results when parents are in the full vigour of life. They should not be too young nor too old, although these terms are often relative, as there are very marked differences in individuals as regards the phenomena of youth or age. Beyond this it is difficult to lay down exact laws. With reference to statutes regulating the age of marriage, seventeen American States have none, but in nine of these common law has fixed the age for girls at twelve years.

The tendency in modern society to postpone the marriage age is not regarded with favour by eugenists. It is largely due to economic causes and is especially noted among the educated and desirable classes. It is highly important that efforts should be made by some sort of social readjustment to render it easy for this class to

SELECTIVE BREEDING 35

marry earlier in life. Good health should be a prerequisite at any age.

Another view is advanced by Casper L. Redfield,[1] who has made an extensive statistical study of heredity. He believes that very early marriages are apt to produce children lacking in stamina and mental power. He considers that as each individual undergoes certain physical and mental changes during life, those conditions which characterize parents at different ages are transmitted to the offspring produced at those ages. This is especially exemplified in mental aptitudes, as the children of youthful parents are usually marked by the characteristics of youth while the children of older parents show more of the characteristics of age. Older parents are thus apt to have intelligent offspring and many historical examples of this are cited, from Aristotle to Benjamin Franklin.

The following quotation will exemplify his belief on this subject,—"The period of adolescence is a period of sexual intensity and passion, and a child born of parents at this age has the sexual instincts abnormally developed, the same as we have aggressiveness from parents of 25, the love of the beautiful from parents of 35, reasoning and practical

[1] *Control of Heredity*—Monarch Book Co.

36　HEREDITY AND CHILD CULTURE

usefulness from parents of 45, and morality and philosophy from parents over 50."

Contrary to Weismann, Redfield believes that traits directly acquired by the efforts of the individual himself can be transmitted. He finally states the following,—"All that you have learned and all that you have accomplished can and will be transmitted to future generations by others through the medium of records. But in whatever measure you have developed your body and your mind by patient and long-continued efforts that measure can be transmitted only by yourself to your descendants, and whatever honour these descendants achieve in the future, that honour will be your honour."

It must be confessed that a discussion on the proper conditions of mating is always largely academic as marriages are usually not contracted by reason but by passion or self-interest. The preliminaries are approached as the result of affinity or liking and not with the idea of breeding in mind. As the race advances in knowledge and control, however, the latter will be kept more in view. After all, it is what to *avoid* in mating that assumes the principal importance.

Some States are now beginning to require a medical examination and certificate before

SELECTIVE BREEDING 37

marriage is permitted. This is good as far as it goes, but it must be remembered that the diseases for which the examination is especially made are not passed along by organic inheritance. They are infections that, in an active state, can be passed directly from one parent to the other, or from mother to child before, during, or after birth. Pathogenic bacteria are not incorporated in the germ plasm itself. Syphilis and tuberculosis are the most important infections that may in this way be passed along. While venereal and constitutional diseases are thus spread by direct infection, they may eventually so poison the germ plasm itself that the offspring will be feeble and ailing although not having a specific disease. The lesson from all this is that candidates for marriage should always be obliged by the State to submit to a thorough medical examination to prove not only their freedom from specific infections but that their systems have not been unduly weakened from previous attacks of constitutional disease. Applicants for marriage licenses should be obliged to prove that they are physically as well as financially fit for marriage,

Perhaps the next great danger consists in the inheritance of various neurotic tendencies,

38   HEREDITY AND CHILD CULTURE

While nervous disease itself may not be passed along, certain abnormal and unstable states may eventuate in various forms of insanity, as well as in feeble-mindedness, epilepsy and mania. These are generally considered to act as Mendelian recessives. Professor Conklin believes there is often an hereditary basis for nervous or phlegmatic temperaments, for emotional, judicial and calculating dispositions, for strength or weakness of will, for tendencies to moral obliquity or rectitude, and for capacity or incapacity for the highest intellectual pursuits. There is great danger of close blood relatives marrying when a neurotic strain runs in the family. When free of this danger, however, evil consequences to the offspring do not always follow.

There is a large class in every community that should in some way be prevented by the State from propagating its kind. The reason for this is readily seen in the danger and expense they put upon the community at large.

The insane, idiotic, blind and deaf mutes tend to increase faster in proportion than the normal healthy population. Paupers and the various grades of criminal population also freely propagate. A careful study of prisoners has shown that a majority are in a condition of

SELECTIVE BREEDING 39

impaired health, that many are in an unsound mental condition and inclined to grave diseases of the neurotic type which tend to modify the physical, mental and moral condition from bad inheritance.

Perhaps the greatest danger exists in the case of feeble-mindedness. It has been estimated that there are 200,000 feeble-minded persons in the United States. Of this large number fully nine-tenths are under no control and thus are able to produce their kind. It is from this vast army that criminals, prostitutes and paupers are recruited. These classes have an imperfect development of the higher areas of the brain and a moral instability that often seems impossible to correct. They cannot adjust themselves to proper social standards and quickly become incorrigible when temptations or unusual demands present themselves. Unfortunately, their condition does not preclude reproduction but rather favours it from lack of conscience and control.

One of the great problems of the day is how to check this tainted stream not only for the good of society but for the defectives themselves. A plan favoured by some is to subject them to sterilization. This has been tried in a limited way, but it need hardly be said there

40 HEREDITY AND CHILD CULTURE

are great social and legal difficulties in the way of its general adoption. A recent judicial decision in Oregon holds that the sterilization law adopted by that State is unconstitutional.

Is there no other way of handling these defectives, who are often as prolific as they are undesirable? Many years ago I advised that they be permanently quarantined.[1] If this were done, in one or two decades they would die out, and the world would be free of its principal source of criminals and defectives. This class should be permanently isolated from the rest of society. According to this aspect, the question of responsibility or punishment does not enter into the question at all. It is simply society protecting itself. Hence a perplexing and uncertain problem is thereby removed. Legislation in Ohio adjudges a person an habitual criminal when convicted of a third offence, under which conviction he may be held for life. This law is based upon sound physiology and psychology. Such a quarantine should be applied to all tramps, cranks and generally worthless beings. Society must do this for protection, not punishment; to avoid their contamination; and, above all, to prevent the propagation of their kind. Advanced sociology

---

[1] "The Survival of the Unfit," *Popular Science Monthly*, June 1892.

SELECTIVE BREEDING 41

will devote its principal energy to preventing the reproduction of the unfit, and, if any are produced, by proper isolation see to it that they do not survive beyond one generation. Here lies the only solution of a very difficult problem,—first, try prevention; next, permanent isolation.

Finally, it is certain that the responsibility of bringing children into the world is usually not taken seriously enough. To produce offspring handicapped by diseased tendencies or without the ability to give them proper nutrition or training is really race suicide that we hear so often condemned. Among 1258 living decendants of Max Jukes, there were 310 paupers, 600 feeble-minded, and over 300 prostitutes. If simply bringing large numbers of children into the world is admirable, certain social and ecclesiastical lawgivers might think that the older Jukes, reprobate though he was, did his duty by the State. It is quality not quantity that is to be sought in children.

If parents cannot properly raise large families, they should not be encouraged to produce them. It is actually found that the poorest and frequently the least desirable elements in the population are apt to have the largest number of children, for which they frequently receive

42 HEREDITY AND CHILD CULTURE

undeserved praise. I once made a study of the size of families in connection with 1,000 children who came under my hospital care in the lower East Side of New York. There were 557 large families, (more than five members) and 443 small families (less that five members) on the list. An interesting point was that the families earning the higher wages were small; while the large families were almost invariably in the low-wage class. In the latter, the income was always insufficient to maintain a proper standard of living. This will be of interest to the advocates of birth control, and certainly, as far as the married among the very poor are concerned, there is much to be said in its favour. There is nothing admirable in bringing forth children who are born to suffering and only destined to fill our hospitals and asylums, whose emaciated little bodies soon find fortunate rest in Potter's field. This is not so much race suicide as race homicide.

CHAPTER V

THE BEGINNING OF LIFE

AN independent life starts by the union of the sperm cell and ovum. The greatest miracle of nature has now taken place,—conception. It has been well said that at the instant of conception the gates of heredity are closed.

It is wonderful to think that by a combination of two tiny cells a life may be inaugurated that can develop into a vigorous adult. When we see a grown child bearing a striking physical resemblance to one or both parents it is hard to realise that this resemblance had its origin in two minute germ cells through which have passed the stream of heredity.

The male cell is microscopic, the relation in size being about as 100,000 to 1 in comparison to the ovum. Yet this spermatozoan, microscopic as it is, yields abundant energy and starts life in the ovum which contains the material to nourish the beginning existence. Dr. Charles Mercier[1] aptly puts it thus,—" My hypothesis

[1] *Lancet* November 8, 1913.

44 HEREDITY AND CHILD CULTURE

is that the contributions of these two elements (sperm cell and germ cell) to the product differ in this way : the female element contributes the substance or matter of the offspring ; the male element contributes the force or energy that animates the matter.   The female element is the coals in the grate ; the male element is the match that sets them alight."

After conception, a series of marvellous changes rapidly takes place.   From the first dawn of life to full development, there is constantly going on a remarkable series of rapid evolutions that are not only fraught with the greatest interest but accompanied by the largest possibilities.

In the course of development before birth, the human embryo passes through different stages of resemblance to a similar period of evolution in the lower animals.   In various earlier stages, the human embryo can hardly be distinguished from the embryonic fish, reptile, and the lower and higher mammals.   The human embryo, however, rapidly passes through these lower stages, accomplishing in a few hours or days a development that required innumerable ages for the lower forms of life and which represented their completed life achievement.   The whole natural history of life is thus sketched and

THE BEGINNING OF LIFE 45

moulded in a growing human fœtus, each step in advance being duly chronicled by a higher stage of evolution, the pedigree of one form going back to simpler previous forms. As geology can trace back the earlier physical conditions of the earth by examining various strata on the surface, so the biologist by studying different stages of growth in the human embryo can see traces of numberless lower forms of life that have long since vanished, each, however, making its humble contribution to the ascending scale. All these phantom lives have had their share, infinitesimal though it be, in forming the acme of animal life,—the human embryo.

As growth progresses, the immature human being rapidly advances from these lower forms, however, until at birth all resemblance to the lower stages of life ceases and the infant gives evidence of the highest possibilities. These phenomena show the human infant to be the microcosm or summing up of all created life. Even at birth the infant is not a completely formed human being, but from this time on the difference from the lower forms of life becomes most startling.

After nine months of intra-uterine life the infant is sufficiently developed to branch forth

46   HEREDITY AND CHILD CULTURE

in an independent existence.   During this period, however, the mother is a trustee not only of her own health but of the well-being and development of the rapidly forming infant.

Pre-Natal Care

Constant oversight should be exercised over the pregnant woman, not only on her own account but in the interest of the unborn child. Control of the pre-natal period has proved to be a most important factor in reducing infant morbidity and mortality.   Owing to a lack of skilled supervision, maternal deaths and deaths of infants from maternal causes have not decreased in proportion to the lessened death rate of later infancy.   The Children's Bureau of Washington reports that in a study of rural areas of six different states, 80 per cent of the mothers have received no trained oversight during pregnancy.   The witty aphorism of Dr. Holmes that the proper time to begin treatment of many diseases is one hundred years before birth might be paraphrased into the idea that an available period of nine months *can* be utilized in trying to produce a healthy infant. Of deaths occurring under one year, over 40 per cent are due to unfavourable congenital conditions.   Of all deaths during the first

THE BEGINNING OF LIFE 47

month of life, 80 per cent. are due to causes associated with prematurity or congenital diseases, deformities or malformations. Thus among all babies dying under one year, over one-third die before they are one month old. Most of these babies die because they are too feeble or sickly to survive, and this in turn may be caused by improper oversight of the mother. It is especially during the latter months of pregnancy that extra care must be observed. Every woman is entitled to adequate supervision up to the time of the birth of her child as well as during and after its birth. The life that comes before birth must have about as much attention as the life that follows birth. Not only for the sake of the child, but a needlessly large mortality on the part of the mothers may thus be avoided.

The importance of this subject is now being recognized and pre-natal clinics are being conducted by departments of health to look after those who cannot afford private advice. Maternal welfare centres, under private management, are also being conducted with excellent results. Every woman who can afford a regular attending physician should be under his constant care during all of this period, instead of waiting until the time of labour is approaching.

48 HEREDITY AND CHILD CULTURE

The importance of proper regulation at this time will be appreciated when we consider an estimate that 20,000 maternal deaths due to child birth and 200,000 deaths of infants occurred during 1920 in the United States. Outside of the stated examinations of various kinds, a quiet, hygienic life is most desirable. In general, the mother should maintain herself in as good a condition of health as possible while she is carrying the child. All the functions of her body must be satisfactorily performed. No social or household duties must be allowed to interfere with this principal business of her life.

At this period it is well for her to thoroughly systematize her life so that the best results will be obtained. Plenty of pure, fresh air is essential. Her living and sleeping rooms must be well ventilated, and she should take the outer air in daily walks or drives, or by sitting much on the piazza during warm weather. Regular exercise is very beneficial, but nothing severe or jolting should be allowed. Plenty of rest and sleep is desirable. The night's sleep should include at least eight hours and more if desired. It is also well to lie down and rest for a season in the middle of the day.

The clothing must be comfortable and loose-

THE BEGINNING OF LIFE 49

fitting, especially avoiding any undue pressure upon the chest or abdomen. Clothing that is so arranged as to be suspended largely from the shoulders is well adapted for this period. Shoes with low heels should be worn, as the high heels in vogue put an undue strain upon the spine and lower abdomen.

There is no scientific proof that special forms of diet have any influence upon the development of the child, but the food should be nourishing and digestible. The free drinking of pure water between meals and at bedtime is beneficial by keeping the kidneys in good working order. The bowels must act once daily and at regular time.

Special care should be given to the breasts and nipples. Breast feeding after birth often fails from lack of early attention. Tender nipples that soon become cracked or sore, or depressed nipples that cannot be grasped by the infant, often result in nursing failures. We must always remember that the loss of breast feeding is an important cause of infant mortality. By gentle massage of the nipples during the last few months of pregnancy, perhaps with cocoa-butter or vaseline, and by using weak alcohol solutions if necessary to toughen the tender skin, we can do much to enable

D

50   HEREDITY AND CHILD CULTURE

the nipple to function well when the time comes.

The influence the mind exerts on the body is recognized by all physicians, and therefore it is well that the future mother should keep as cheerful and composed as possible. To this end, she should be kept from undue cares and worries, and have as bright surroundings as circumstances will allow. Strong mental excitement and unrepressed emotions have a bad effect at this time. It is right to add, however, that the bugbear of "maternal impressions" producing some subtle and disastrous influence on the unborn infant has no scientific basis.

In a general way, the care of the future child is taking place during the whole of the previous life of the mother, but in a very special way is such care obvious while she is carrying the baby. The problem of the child begins with conception and ends with adolescence, and of all these periods that of pregnancy is one of the most neglected.

Modern asepsis has robbed child birth of much of its dangers for the mother, but still the greatest care must be exercised at this time. Danger to the child often results from too great a prolongation of labour. As a consequence of long pressure, a rupture of some of the delicate

THE BEGINNING OF LIFE 51

blood vessels on the surface of the brain may ensue and the child thereby be handicapped for life. Holmes once described the female pelvis as the triumphal arch through which the new-born infant first passed to greet the world. If this arch is too narrow for comfortable exit, it may require some skilful surgery to deliver the child intact.

CHAPTER VI

THE DEVELOPING PERIOD

THE practical problem of evolution consists in regulating biological heredity as far as possible, and then in trying to produce conditions that will enable social heredity to act to the best advantage.

This must start with an inquiry as to the usual physical and mental characteristics that go with a good heredity, biological or social, or both. In other words, what may be considered an average normal condition for the infant and growing child? In this way we may determine, at least, whether a favourable social heredity is present in each case. We cannot alter biological heredity, but we can and should aim to correct a faulty social heredity if such exists. The latter may be shown by physical or mental under-development.

Growth During Infancy

The infant should start life with rapid growth. During the first year there is a greater

THE DEVELOPING PERIOD 53

proportional growth to initial size than at any other time of life. This is due to an extremely rapid proliferation of body cells and not to cell enlargement that comes after two or three years. Any condition that interferes with growth, such as an insufficient diet or intercurrent illness, should be averted by all the care that can be rendered. It has been observed that colds, bronchitis, ear trouble, indigestion or constipation will inhibit growth when these conditions last for two or three weeks.

It is important to have a record of birth weight in every case. The male infant usually weighs a little more than the female. In a series of 200 cases that I examined, the males weighed from six to eight pounds, and the females from five and a half to seven pounds. As many of these infants were born in institutions, the averages of light weight were fairly large. Seven pounds may be considered a good average birth weight, although this may be exceeded by vigorous infants. As far as initial weight may be considered a gauge of vitality, six and a half pounds will show a good vitality, five and a half pounds a rather poor one, and from four to five pounds a very poor vitality at the start.

Some infants are born with small bones, per-

54 HEREDITY AND CHILD CULTURE

haps in this respect resembling one or both parents. The birth weight of such an infant, as well as that attained later, will be less than that of a baby having a larger bony framework. Different races, as well as families, show considerable variation in this respect. Needless alarm is sometimes excited if the physician or mother merely consider averages that are taken from a different class or community and hence do not particularly apply to the baby under consideration. This fact may be considered in connection with relative weights and heights at all ages. In every case, the extremely rapid growth of the infant after birth makes careful observation of all the phenomena connected therewith not only interesting but important.

During the first few days there is generally a loss of from four to six ounces, after which there should be a steady gain. It must be remembered, however, that babies are apt to gain irregularly at short intervals. One day the infant may show a gain of an ounce and the next day a quarter of that amount while doing perfectly well. Again, the weight may remain stationary for a day or so and then jump up two ounces in twenty-four hours. There should at least be an average weekly gain during the first five months of about four and a half ounces to

THE DEVELOPING PERIOD 55

seven ounces, and from five to twelve months of about two and a half to four and a half ounces.

The infant should double its birth weight at five or six months, and treble it at twelve to fifteen months. The weighing should be done by the same person either on grocer's scales or lever scales specially constructed for infants. Daily weighings are often deceptive and undesirable. During the first six months once a week is sufficient, and in the second six months once in two weeks is often enough in cases that are doing well. Careful records should be kept, and charting is convenient for reference.

The length of the new-born baby is slightly greater in the male than in the female. In private practice, with healthy parents, the length will average about twenty inches. Growth in length is most rapid during the first month, a little less so during the second month, and rapidly decreases during each succeeding month. During the first year there is a growth in length of about eight inches, and in the second year of about three and a half inches.

Just after birth, the trunk, arms, legs and head have peculiar conformations. The body is of an elliptical shape, with the widest part at about the centre over the liver, in the region of

56 HEREDITY AND CHILD CULTURE

the lower ribs. The two ends of the ellipse, represented by the chest and pelvis, are relatively small and not well developed. The arms are stronger and better developed than the legs. During intra-uterine life the baby is placed in a sort of squatting position with the legs drawn up and curled inward. This explains why the legs of the young infant are not straight but show a decided bowing inward. The soles of the feet also tend to point inward. The head is larger than the chest at this time, with a very short neck, and the baby assumes a position of general flexion.

While infants at birth may vary in size, each individual should develop in proper proportion, the various parts of the body bearing a symmetrical relationship to one another. Thus the circumference of the head is greater than the circumference of the chest, and remains so up to the middle of the first year, when they begin to approximate in size. At the end of the first year the chest should expand to a greater circumference than the head. If later than this time the circumference of the head remains greater than that of the chest, it is an indication of faulty development. The sutures of the skull should be ossified by the end of the sixth month, and the opening in the head known as

THE DEVELOPING PERIOD 57

the *anterior fontanelle* closes from the sixteenth to the eighteenth month. Any deformities of the head due to prolonged pressure and difficult labours are usually overcome during the first few weeks. After birth and with increase in age, there is noted a gradual and steady enlargement of the great circumference of the skull, and, from this, of its estimated volume. Although no intellectual growth can be said to take place under two years, there should be an active evolution of the front of the brain with increase of the perceptions. The first rapid growth of the brain after birth is more in bulk than in the size and complexity of its convolutions. Hence in early infancy the higher centres have but a slight development and function. With proper evolution, the convolutions grow and become arranged in functional groups, which groups, by their development, alter and modify the shape of the infantile skull. If the skull is small or improperly shaped in any part, the brain in such area is imperfectly developing. A certain amount of asymmetry is, however, found in all skulls as in other structures of the body and, unless very marked, has no great significance.

The principle of biology that the development of the individual reproduces on a small scale the development of the race is well shown

58 HEREDITY AND CHILD CULTURE

in the infant's brain. The higher centres and the association fibres are developed late in the child; they are likewise the latest acquirements of the race. The lower and more fundamental animal traits are transmitted by inheritance in greater degree than the higher ones.

In the human being, the brain assumes overmastering importance in the scheme of evolution, hence its proper growth and development are relatively of much more importance than that of other parts of the body. The extremely rapid evolution of the brain during infancy, and the fact that the future efficiency and well-being of the child depend largely upon its normal and healthy growth renders the study of the infantile head of great interest. As the skull is fairly representative of the brain during the years of its first development, measurements taken during infancy are more instructive as to brain size and evolution than those taken in later years. The skull changes considerably in its proportions during the first years of life, and then more slowly up to the end of the seventh year when it has very nearly attained its full size. At birth, the circumference of the head averages from thirteen to fourteen inches; at the end of the second year, about eighteen inches ; at the seventh year, about twenty and

THE DEVELOPING PERIOD 59

a half inches, and at the completion of growth twenty-two or more inches.

The spinal column is curved but very flexible. In early infancy, the so-called normal curves are not developed above the pelvis but there is one long curve in the shape of a general convexity. As the child grows older, the spine becomes less flexible and more rigid with increased power in the spinal muscles. There is, however, much more flexibility all through early life than obtains in later years.

In the musculature, the greatest relative strength is shown in the hands and arms for a time after birth. At about three months, the muscles of the neck have developed sufficiently to allow the infant to hold up its head in an uncertain way. At the seventh or eighth months, the muscles of the back have become strengthened so that the baby can sit up, and shortly after this it may be allowed to creep. Free play should be given to the muscles of the arms and legs from the first, as muscular and body development are thereby encouraged. The bones of the leg thus grow and straighten out, but this will be checked if the infant is allowed to sustain the weight of the body too soon. The average baby should not be allowed to stand before the twelfth month. Efforts to walk may be encouraged from then on to the fifteenth or sixteenth months. When walking has been established, the legs should be straight.

The process of dentition begins early in intra-uterine life. The cutting of the temporary or milk teeth usually begins about the sixth or seventh month and should be completed at the end of infancy.

It must be remembered that a healthy infant will always grow both in height and weight. While increase in weight is properly regarded as evidence of good development, it is possible that relatively too much starch or sugar in the diet may produce fat at the expense of bone, muscle and gland. Firmness of tissues and proper growth of the long bones must thus be considered in connection with increase in weight.

HEIGHT AND WEIGHT OF WHITE INFANTS

	White Boys		White Girls	
Age	Height (inches)	Weight (pounds)	Height (inches)	Weight (pounds)
Under 1 month	$21\frac{1}{8}$	$9\frac{1}{8}$	$20\frac{7}{8}$	$8\frac{5}{8}$
3 months	$24\frac{1}{2}$	$14\frac{1}{8}$	24	13
6 months	$26\frac{3}{4}$	$17\frac{1}{2}$	$26\frac{1}{8}$	$16\frac{1}{4}$
9 months	$28\frac{1}{4}$	$19\frac{5}{8}$	$27\frac{5}{8}$	$18\frac{1}{2}$
12 months	$29\frac{1}{2}$	$21\frac{3}{8}$	$28\frac{7}{8}$	20
15 months	$30\frac{5}{8}$	$22\frac{3}{4}$	$30\frac{1}{8}$	$21\frac{3}{8}$
18 months	$31\frac{3}{4}$	$24\frac{1}{8}$	$31\frac{1}{4}$	$22\frac{3}{4}$
21 months	$32\frac{3}{4}$	$25\frac{1}{2}$	$32\frac{1}{4}$	$24\frac{1}{8}$
24 months	$33\frac{5}{8}$	$26\frac{5}{8}$	$33\frac{1}{8}$	$25\frac{1}{8}$

These figures are based on measurements of a very large number of infants in whom no serious defects were reported, collected by the

THE DEVELOPING PERIOD 61

Federal Children's Bureau.[1] They closely agree with measurements of 3,448 normal babies in 23 states prepared by Mr. F. S. Crum for the American Medical Association.

Conserving Infant Life

In working for Infants we shall be enabled to get an important side light on general social conditions. The infant and little child have always offered the best approach to a study of both medical and social problems. They connect directly with all lines of social inquiry,— housing, food, parenthood, the wage problem, faulty hygiene in tenement or town, education and every other factor in community life.

One of the most fruitful social movements of the day is thus connected with the saving and conserving of infant life. There has been a marked lessening both in morbidity and mortality of infants as the result of these efforts. Thus in New York City there has been a reduction in the infant mortality rate from 273.6 per 1,000 children born in 1885 to 81.6 in 1919, and 71.1 in 1921. This decline has been aided by such factors as more breast feeding, baby health station service, careful oversight of cows'

[1] U. S. Department of Labour, Children's Bureau. No. 84.

62 HEREDITY AND CHILD CULTURE

milk, visiting nurses, improvement in municipal sanitation and better control over communicable disease. A lower death-rate always predicates less sickness and more vigorous vitality in the

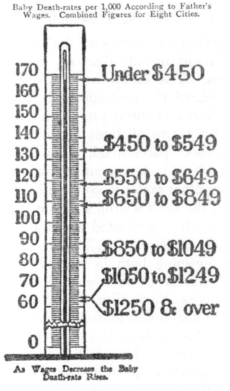

Baby Death-rates per 1,000 According to Father's Wages. Combined Figures for Eight Cities.

As Wages Decrease the Baby Death-rate Rises.

infants who live. While deaths among older babies have decreased, the number of infant

THE DEVELOPING PERIOD 63

deaths during the first month has not lessened, but at times has even increased, which shows that the pre-natal and natal periods have not been equally watched. The reason that five times as many babies die in the first month as in the second, and fourteen times as many as in the twelfth, is that parents are unhealthy or the mothers were not given proper oversight and care during pregnancy. This early mortality can be much reduced by instructing the mother how to stimulate breast feeding during the first months after birth, and by better methods of hygiene and artificial feeding.

Infants and little children are always the most sensitive to bad environment. They are likewise the first to suffer from poor economic conditions. The Federal Children's Bureau has shown graphically how the infant death-rate goes up as wages go down.

In a study of 3700 cases of serious illness in infants and little children treated in the hospital in a long series of years, I [1] found the causes along three broad lines,—insufficient earnings, bad housing and ignorance of the parents. Poverty and sickness too often go hand in hand. The Charity Organization Society has

[1] "The Relation Between the Child and Hospital Social Service "— *Journal of the American Medical Association*, July 23, 1921,

64 HEREDITY AND CHILD CULTURE

found that fully two-thirds of the cases of poverty it is called on to investigate depend, directly or indirectly, on sickness. There is a shifting and alternating relationship of cause and effect between them. It is interesting to note how this vicious circle works at different ages. Thus while in adult years, sickness is one of the principal causes of poverty, in childhood poverty is one of the principal causes of sickness.

It is evident that infant salvage is closely inter-related with economic and social conditions. To save the baby and conserve the beginning life we may have to go far afield in a study of life conditions. About 300,000 babies under one year die every year in this country. There is still much to be done. Putting it in another way, it has been estimated that in the United States twelve babies out of every hundred, under the age of twelve months, die every year, In the great World War less than two men out of every hundred were killed in battle. During this time, accordingly, a soldier in the trenches was six times as safe as the baby in the slums. This shows that social heredity,—in other words environment,—has yet much to do in conserving infant life. A most beneficial and far-reaching element in this work is that

THE DEVELOPING PERIOD 65

general social amelioration must both accompany and follow these efforts. The baby may yet lead the way in social reconstruction.

E

CHAPTER VII

THE PRE-SCHOOL AGE

In a study of the developing period of life, two gaps have occurred in which sufficient over-sight has not been given. Attention has already been directed to the first of these periods,—the time before birth, The second comparatively neglected period is the pre-school age,—from two to six years. Boards of health and welfare stations have concentrated on the infant with a result of lowering infant morbidity and mortality ; school physicians and nurses have given oversight to older children, but the pre-school child has fallen between these two periods. Even well-to-do people, who do not depend on public agencies for medical over-sight, are apt to give too little attention to the child before entrance into school. The baby is so helpless that constant advice is sought, and now most private as well as public schools have physicians who exercise some oversight over child development, but the little run-about is too often left to his own devices.

THE PRE-SCHOOL AGE 67

This is a most unfortunate state of affairs, because we are here dealing with a most important age. During infancy growth is steady and rapid, but in childhood it is relatively slower and takes place more in cycles. It depends very largely upon good heredity and a healthy, well nourished state during the first years of life. Biological researches show that favourable embryonic conditions and good nutrition during the earliest years have the greatest influence in determining the full height and development of the individual. If a child is fortunate in its birth and is well nourished up to the fifth or sixth years, there will probably be a healthy growth thereafter, as, even if there are poor conditions later on, nature will probably be able to compensate and make up for them. Each person has a certain normal size to attain, which will usually be reached if the first years have been favourable. Nothing will completely make up, however, for early unfavourable conditions.

The following table that I have prepared from data collected by the Federal Children's Bureau will give some idea of the development that was found among a large number of American children from two to six years of age.

68   HEREDITY AND CHILD CULTURE

HEIGHT AND WEIGHT OF WHITE CHILDREN (2 TO 6 YEARS)

| | White Boys | | White Girls | |
Age	Height (inches)	Weight (pounds)	Height (inches)	Weight (pounds)
25 months	$33\frac{7}{8}$	27	$33\frac{5}{8}$	$25\frac{1}{2}$
3 years	$36\frac{5}{8}$	$30\frac{3}{4}$	$36\frac{1}{4}$	$29\frac{1}{2}$
4 years	$39\frac{1}{4}$	$34\frac{1}{2}$	$38\frac{7}{8}$	$33\frac{1}{2}$
5 years	$41\frac{5}{8}$	$38\frac{1}{4}$	$41\frac{3}{8}$	$36\frac{7}{8}$
6 years	$43\frac{7}{8}$	$41\frac{3}{4}$	$43\frac{5}{8}$	$40\frac{1}{2}$

In a study of nearly 40,000 children of pre-school age in Iowa, it was found that the boys from birth to six years were uniformly taller and heavier at all ages than the girls. It was also noted that the percentages of total stature and weight at six years showed that the height doubled in these cases during the first six years after birth and the weight increased four times. The rural Iowa children were above the urban ones in stature and weight from birth to six years.

The years of the pre-school age, before six, represent a critical time in reference to future development. The frequent magnitude of the problem may be realized when we consider the estimate that there are about half a million children of the pre-school age in New York City. These children should all be carefully examined twice a year in order to recognize any condition or defect that can usually be corrected at the start.

It is now believed by many observers that

THE PRE-SCHOOL AGE 69

numerous defects and degenerations of later life have their real origin from some infection or other unfortunate condition during the first few years. For example, it is held that few adults have escaped infection by the tubercle bacillus, but the disease becomes latent and harmless unless a diminished resistance has been inherited or the general health much depressed. It is further believed that the original focus of infection is nearly always started during the early years. In making autopsies on mal-nourished children in the hospital, I have nearly always found some tuberculous focus even in cases of death from other causes. The first inception of this insidious malady almost always comes at the beginning of life. If the general vitality is conserved, however, nothing but a harmless encapsulated spot will usually remain, but at the same time every effort must be made to keep the body from infection.

What is true of tuberculosis is true of all other infections. Measles and whooping-cough are two of the most dangerous diseases of this age as regards ultimate effects. This is the most susceptible period of life to all communicable disease. Young protoplasm affords a virgin and favourable soil for the growth of

70 HEREDITY AND CHILD CULTURE

bacteria and the spread of all kinds of virus. In this respect, the pre-school child is much more susceptible than the infant or the older child. One of the common diseases of early life, diphtheria, well shows this peculiarity. It has been found that over 90 per cent. of new-born infants are immune to this disease, 70 per cent. during the first year, while somewhat over half fail to contract the disease on exposure later in childhood. Immunity from infection of most kinds seems to be conferred upon the baby by inheritance from its mother, and this lasts for varying periods but not long after infancy.

Another fact to be considered is that the run-about is naturally more exposed from moving around and possibly coming in close contact with scarlet fever, measles, whooping-cough, and other communicable diseases. While these affections may not kill, they frequently leave sequelæ that handicap the future life of the individual.

Other common conditions that frequently start and develop during this period of life are enlarged and diseased tonsils, adenoids at the vault of the pharnyx that interfere with respiration, and sluggishly inflamed lymph glands in various parts of the body.

THE PRE-SCHOOL AGE 71

Beginning caries of the teeth from insufficient care may also have serious consequences. The temporary teeth need special attention not only in starting proper mastication, but because the permanent teeth are lodged in the jaw just above them and the latter are liable to become affected by disease of the former. Good digestion is dependent on good teeth, and various constitutional affections are known to come from disease and pus pockets about the roots of the teeth.

The various gastro-intestinal diseases, from careless feeding and poor hygiene, are very common with the little child. A careful oversight of the infant's bottle too often gives place to later laxity in feeding. The selection and administration of food is often left to ignorant servants or nurses. As a result, various forms of malnutrition and even deficiency diseases may ensue. Anæmia, mal-development, and various nerve affections are apt to follow along in this path.

This is the time to develop a correct posture, and the child must be taught how to stand and sit erect, as such habits last through life. Minor curvatures of the spine, which is very supple, are a common cause of poor carriage and can easily be corrected at the beginning.

72 HEREDITY AND CHILD CULTURE

The close connection between the pre-school child and the over-sight that must come in the future has been well expressed by Dr. Sobel of the New York Board of Health,—" The Bureau of Child Hygiene has always felt that the best time to take care of the child's health is before he enters school, and that preventive and remedial measures, undertaken at this time would do much toward the elimination or diminution of physical defects, and place him in a sound, physical condition upon school entrance, to say nothing of the favourable effect upon his growth and development prior to school age. In fact, the Bureau feels that proper supervision during the pre-school age bears the same relation to school medical inspection that proper pre-natal instruction and supervision bear to infant mortality. Just as any decided reduction in infant mortality must come through the reduction of deaths from congenital diseases and deaths during the first month of life, through a constructive pre-natal programme, so any material reduction in the percentage of physical defects found in school children, and a betterment of their general well-being must come through the care of the children before their entrance into school."

CHAPTER VIII

THE SCHOOL CHILD

THE child of school age enters into a long period which should be one of healthy growth. It includes the time from six years to and through adolescence. To be healthy, a child must grow both in height and weight, but this does not usually take place in a steady and uninterrupted manner, but rather in cycles that may be longer or shorter.

The two principal periods of acceleration of growth occur during the second dentition, or when the permanent teeth begin to be cut, and at the beginning of adolescence. This roughly corresponds, first, with the period from six to nine years in boys and girls, and, second, from eleven to thirteen in girls and from fourteen to sixteen in boys. This cycle of increase in height should precede and soon be followed by an increase in weight. In boys there is apt to be a slackening in growth before the approach of puberty, usually between the tenth and eleventh years. Boys grow quicker in height

74 HEREDITY AND CHILD CULTURE

than girls till between ten and eleven years, when girls become taller until about fourteen at which time boys again take the lead. Girls gain in weight up to ten years in about the same ratio as boys, but they then are apt to increase more rapidly than boys up to about the fifteenth year, when the boys attain a quicker rate and are then permanently heavier. There also tends to be some variation in growth in different seasons. There is usually more rapid increase in height during summer, and in weight through the fall and spring months. This may be explained by the fact that summer is vacation time with possibilities of abundant outdoor air and plenty of pleasant exercise.

Whenever there is a rapid increase in height, the child is apt to grow thin and anæmic, as the making of bone quickly uses up the red corpuscles of the blood. These children become nervous and irritable, requiring extra care at home and school. Such supervision must concern itself with a carefully selected diet, plenty of rest, and the avoidance of intellectual over-stimulation. These children must never be pushed at school, and it may even be necessary to remove them for a time if they are worried by their studies.

It has been proved from examinations of many

THE SCHOOL CHILD 75

school children that, as a rule, the heaviest and tallest, or those with the best physique, stand highest in their classes and show the best intellectual development. Hence, if a child is poorly nourished or undeveloped, the best thing, even for his intellectual growth, is to focus attention on his body for a time and let his mind be temporarily neglected. Competitive examinations at the end of the school year, after the fatigue of the winter's work, coming at a time when growth is usually most active in a child, too often result in nervous exhaustion.

Proper growth in the school child is measured by a study of the relation of height and weight. This gives a truer insight into normal conditions than simply taking the average height and weight of a large number of children and constructing a table to be used as a standard. The latter plan has usually been followed but is subject to certain inaccuracies that may cause undue anxiety on the part of parents and teachers. The manner and degree of increase in height and weight depend to a certain extent upon race and climate, as well as on the size and physique of the parents. It is thus evident that, although these average tables are of value, no absolute rules can be given for comparison that will always apply to every child.

76   HEREDITY AND CHILD CULTURE

A satisfactory table has been compiled by Dr. Thomas D. Wood and is used by the Child Health Organization and the U.S. Government publications.

Weigh on the same date each month about the same hour of the day. Weights and measures should be taken without shoes and in only the usual indoor clothes. Boys should remove their coats.

Here is arranged a sliding scale of the relation of height to weight, according to age, which affords a satisfactory working basis for reference. These measurements can easily be taken by parent or teacher once or twice a year and a fairly satisfactory guide to proper development thus obtained, allowance for individual variations having been made.

The following are some of the conclusions reached after an extensive and thorough study of Iowa school children,[1]—" The weight—height index is the most practical criterion of normal growth in robustness and, other conditions being normal, in general nutrition."

With regard to height,—" For boys and girls from six to eighteen years of age there is a slight adolescence acceleration in height and weight. * * * * As a rule tall boys and tall

[1] *Studies in Child Welfare*—University of Iowa—1921.

THE SCHOOL CHILD

girls reach their periods of maximum adolescent stature earlier than do short ones. * * * If there is retardation before adolescence, the tendency is to show a rapid acceleration during adolescence as a compensating factor. * * * Tall children at any age remain relatively tall under normal conditions. Growth in height is so comparatively uniform for each individual that the growth curve enables one to prophesy with a high degree of accuracy how tall a young child will be at subsequent years. Growth in height is affected by the formation and removal of adenoids. Prolonged disease history retards normal growth in stature. * * * There is a great probability that a tall boy or girl at six years will be a tall boy or girl at twelve years of age ; a tall boy or girl at nine or ten will be tall at fifteen or sixteen years of age. * * * For height boys have a greater variability than girls at all ages between seven and seventeen, except at twelve and seventeen ; at thirteen they are the same. Boys fluctuate more in variability in height than girls."

The following are some of the conclusions reached as to weight,—"There is more individual variation in growth in weight than in growth in height. Pre-adolescent acceleration in growth in weight precedes as a rule the pre-

HEIGHT and WEIGHT TABLE for BOYS

Height Inches	5 Yrs	6 Yrs	7 Yrs	8 Yrs	9 Yrs	10 Yrs	11 Yrs	12 Yrs	13 Yrs	14 Yrs	15 Yrs	16 Yrs	17 Yrs	18 Yrs
39	35	36	37											
40	37	38	39											
41	39	40	41											
42	41	42	43	44										
43	43	44	45	46										
44	45	46	47											
45	47	47	48	48	49									
46	48	49	50	50	51									
47		51	52	53	54									
48		53	54	55	55	56	57							
49		55	56	57	58	59								
50			58	59	60	60	61	62						
51			60	61	62	63	64	65						
52			62	63	64	65	67	68						
53				66	67	68	69	70	71					
54				69	70	71	72	73	74					
55					73	74	75	76	77	78				
56					77	78	79	80	81	82				
57						81	82	83	84	85	86			
58						84	85	86	87	88	90	91		
59						87	88	89	90	92	94	96	97	
60						91	92	93	94	97	99	101	102	
61							95	97	99	102	104	106	108	110
62							100	102	104	106	109	111	113	116
63							105	107	109	111	114	115	117	119
64								113	115	117	118	119	120	122
65									120	122	123	124	125	126
66									125	126	127	128	129	130
67									130	131	132	133	134	135
68									134	135	136	137	138	139
69									138	139	140	141	142	143
70										142	144	145	146	147
71										147	149	150	151	152
72										152	154	155	156	157
73										157	159	160	161	162
74										162	164	165	166	167
75											169	170	171	172
76											174	175	176	177

PREPARED BY DR. THOMAS D. WOOD

About what a BOY should Gain Each Month

AGE		AGE	
5 to 8 ... ... 6 oz.		12 to 16 ... ... 16 oz.	
8 to 12 ... ... 8 oz.		16 to 18 ... ... 8 oz.	

HEIGHT and WEIGHT TABLE for GIRLS[1]

Height Inches	5 Yrs	6 Yrs	7 Yrs	8 Yrs	9 Yrs	10 Yrs	11 Yrs	12 Yrs	13 Yrs	14 Yrs	15 Yrs	16 Yrs	17 Yrs	18 Yrs
39	34	35	36											
40	36	37	38											
41	38	39	40											
42	40	41	42	43										
43	42	42	43	44										
44	44	45	45	46										
45	46	47	47	48	49									
46	48	48	49	50	51									
47		49	50	51	52	53								
48		51	52	53	54	55	56							
49		53	54	55	56	57	58							
50			56	57	58	59	60	61						
51			59	60	61	62	63	64						
52			62	63	64	65	66	67						
53				66	67	68	68	69	70					
54				68	69	70	71	72	73					
55					72	73	74	75	76	76				
56						76	77	78	79	80	81			
57							81	82	83	84	85	86		
58							85	86	87	88	89	90	91	
59							89	90	91	93	94	95	96	98
60							94	95	97	99	100	102	104	106
61							99	101	102	104	106	108	109	111
62							104	106	107	109	111	113	114	115
63							109	111	112	113	115	117	118	119
64								115	117	118	119	120	121	122
65								117	119	120	122	123	124	125
66								119	121	122	124	126	127	128
67									124	126	127	128	129	130
68									126	128	130	132	133	134
69									129	131	133	135	136	137
70										134	136	138	139	140
71										138	140	142	143	144
72											145	147	148	149

PREPARED BY DR. THOMAS D. WOOD

About what a GIRL should Gain Each Month

AGE		AGE	
5 to 8	6 oz.	14 to 16	8 oz.
8 to 11	8 oz.	16 to 18	4 oz.
11 to 14	12 oz.		

[1] *Copyright 1918, by Child Health Organization.*

80   HEREDITY AND CHILD CULTURE

adolescent acceleration in growth in height. The pre-adolescent acceleration in growth in weight is earlier, chronologically, for the tall boys and girls than for the short ones. Growth in weight is affected by disease history and the growth and removal of adenoids. * * * The heavy boy or girl at six or nine or ten will be a heavy boy or girl six years later. * * * For weight boys have greater variability except at the ages of nine to thirteen, inclusive, and at sixteen and seventeen. Girls also fluctuate more in variability in weight than boys."

These data represent conclusions reached after an intensive study of a fairly homogeneous class of white American school children in that state.

Many years ago tables of the results of widespread and extensive observations throughout the world were published by the *American Journal of Psychology*.[1] It may be of interest to reproduce two of them here for record and reference.

Apparent stupidity or bad mentality in school children is often the result of physical causes that can and should be removed. Dr.

[1] April, 1898.

THE SCHOOL CHILD 81

Josephine Baker in writing on child health quotes the following :

The New York State Department of Health has published the following figures giving the estimated defects in the 22,000,000 children of the United States:

At least 200,000 (1 per cent.) are mentally defective;

At least 250,000 (over 1 per cent.) are affected with organic heart disease;

At least 1,000,000 (5 per cent.) have now or have had tuberculosis;

At least 1,000,000 (5 per cent.) are unable to hear properly and because this condition is unrecognized many of these children have the undeserved reputation of being mentally defective;

At least 5,000,000 (25 per cent.) have defective eyes;

At least 1 out of every 5 of these children is undernourished;

From 3,000,000 to 5,000,000 (15 per cent. to 25 per cent.) have adenoids, diseased tonsils or other glandular defects;

From 2,000,000 to 4,000,000 (10 per cent. to 20 per cent.) have weak foot arches, weak spines or other joint defects; and

From 11,000,000 to 16,000,000 (50 per cent. to 75 per cent.) have defective teeth.

Most of these defects or diseases are either preventable or remediable if discovered early enough and if the proper treatment is given. When are we going to learn that it is poor economy to neglect the child in school and then care for him during his adult years because of some disability ?

F

Age	Boston (Bowditch). 13,691 boys, 10,304 girls.		St. Louis (Porter). 16,285 boys, 18,069 girls; age nearest birthday.		Milwaukee (G. W. Peckham). 4,773 boys, 4,891 girls.		Oakland. Number not stated.		Worcester (West). 3,250 children.		New Haven (Gilbert). About 50 of each sex for each age.	
	M.	F.	M.	F.	M.	F.	M.	F.	M.	F.	M.	F.
$4\frac{1}{2}$ years ...	....	....	....	....	39.98	39.65	....	....	....	....	....	....
$5\frac{1}{2}$ years ...	41.57	41.29	....	....	42.28	41.72	....	....	43.2	42.3	....	....
$6\frac{1}{2}$ years ...	43.75	43.35	42.9	42.4	44.08	43.78	44.1	44.4	44.4	43.8	45.0	44.9
$7\frac{1}{2}$ years ...	45.74	45.52	44.9	44.5	46.09	45.93	45.0	44.9	46.1	46.3	47.1	46.9
$8\frac{1}{2}$ years ...	47.76	47.58	46.9	46.6	48.05	47.59	47.6	46.8	48.2	47.9	48.9	48.4
$9\frac{1}{2}$ years ...	49.69	49.37	49.0	48.7	50.00	49.81	49.3	49.2	50.0	49.8	51.2	50.8
$10\frac{1}{2}$ years ...	51.68	51.34	50.7	50.6	51.85	51.89	51.9	51.5	52.8	52.3	53.0	52.8
$11\frac{1}{2}$ years ...	53.33	53.42	52.7	52.4	53.76	53.5	53.5	53.9	54.6	53.9	55.9	54.6
$12\frac{1}{2}$ years ...	55.1	55.9	54.4	54.8	55.0	56.5	55.1	56.6	56.3	57.0	57.0	57.9
$13\frac{1}{2}$ years ...	57.2	58.2	56.3	57.7	57.5	58.7	56.8	60.0	58.1	58.2	58.8	60.4
$14\frac{1}{2}$ years ...	59.9	59.9	58.3	59.3	59.9	60.5	59.7	61.2	60.7	60.5	59.3	61.4
$15\frac{1}{2}$ years ...	62.3	61.1	61.0	61.0	62.3	61.6	61.8	61.9	63.9	61.8	62.8	62.5
$16\frac{1}{2}$ years ...	65.0	61.6	63.1	62.0	65.1	62.2	64.5	62.7	65.3	62.4	65.7	62.5
$17\frac{1}{2}$ years ...	66.2	61.9	65.0	62.7	66.6	62.9	67.1	62.7	66.3	62.8	67.1	63.6
$18\frac{1}{2}$ years ...	66.7	61.9	....	62.8	....	62.5	67.6	63.2	66.9	62.6	....	....
$19\frac{1}{2}$ years ...	....	....	....	62.4	....	....	....	....	67.4	62.7	....	....
$20\frac{1}{2}$ years ...	....	....	....	....	....	....	....	....	68.5	62.6	....	....
$21\frac{1}{2}$ years ...	....	....	....	....	....	....	....	....	67.1	62.7	....	....

AVERAGE HEIGHT (IN INCHES) OF CHILDREN IN VARIOUS CITIES AND COUNTRIES OF THE WORLD

Age	Iowa (Gilbert) About 50 of each sex for each age.		Pennsylvania (Hall), 2,434 males (nude).		Moscow (Erisman), 3,212 boys, 1,495 girls.		Sweden Commission (Key), 15,000 boys, 3,000 girls.		Denmark Commission (Hestel), 17,134 boys, 11,250 girls.		England (Roberts), Over 10,000 males.	
	M.	F.	M.	F.	M.	F.	M.	F.	M.	F.	M.	F.
4½ years ...	......	......	......	......	......	......	......	......	......	......	......	......
5½ years ...											41·2	......
6½ years ...	45·0	44·6	......	......	......	......	45·6	44·5	44·1	44·1	43·2	......
7½ years ...	47·8	46·8	......	......	44·1	43·9	47·6	45·7	45·3	45·3	45·0	......
8½ years ...	49·6	49·2	......	......	46·4	45·8	49·6	48·4	47·2	47·2	47·0	......
9½ years ...	51·3	51·3	51·2	......	48·3	47·1	51·6	50·0	49·2	49·2	49·2	......
10½ years ...	53·3	53·0	53·9	......	51·5	49·2	52·4	52·0	51·2	51·2	50·5	......
11½ years ...	55·2	54·5	55·1	......	53·4	51·1	53·5	53·9	53·1	52·4	51·5	......
12½ years ...	57·1	58·0	56·7	......	55·2	52·3	55·1	56·3	54·3	54·3	53·0	......
13½ years ...	58·7	59·2	61·0	......	57·2	54·5	56·7	58·3	56·3	57·5	55·9	......
14½ years ...	61·7	61·7	62·3	......	59·1	57·4	58·7	60·2	58·7	59·4	57·8	......
15½ years ...	64·7	63·3	65·3	......	61·6	......	61·4	61·8	61·4	60·6	60·7	......
16½ years ...	66·7	63·3	66·5	......	63·5	......	63·8	62·6	64·6	62·6	62·9	......
17½ years ...	68·2	64·5	67·1	......	64·6	......	65·7	63·0	65·7	......	64·5	......
18½ years ...	68·6	64·6	67·3	......	......	......	66·9	63·0	66·9	......	65·5	......
19½ years ...	69·0	64·6	67·5	......			67·3	63·8	66·9	......	66·0	......
20½ years ...	......	......	67·6	......			67·7	63·0	......	......	66·3	......
21½ years ...	......	......	97·6	......	......	......	......	......	......	......	......	......

AVERAGE WEIGHT (IN POUNDS) OF CHILDREN IN VARIOUS CITIES AND COUNTRIES OF THE WORLD

Age	Boston. (Bowditch). 15,681 boys, 10,904 girls.		St. Louis. (Porter). 16,295 boys, 18,059 girls; age nearest birthday.		Milwaukee. (G. W. Peckham). 4,722 boys, 4,891 girls.		Oakland. Number not stated.		Worcester. (West). 3,250 children.		New Haven. (Gilbert). About 50 of each sex for each age.	
	M.	F.	M.	F.	M.	F.	M.	F.	M.	F.	M.	F.
$3\frac{1}{2}$ years ...	......	......	......	......	......	......	......	......	......	......	......	......
$4\frac{1}{2}$ years ...	......	......	......	......	......	......	......	......	......	......	......	......
$5\frac{1}{2}$ years ...	41.1	39.7	......	......	38.8	36.3	......	......	......	......	......	......
$6\frac{1}{2}$ years ...	45.2	43.3	43.7	41.7	41.1	40.0	......	......	42.63	39.36	......	......
$7\frac{1}{2}$ years ...	49.1	47.5	47.8	45.9	44.8	43.1	47.6	45.9	46.04	43.70	46.8	44.3
$8\frac{1}{2}$ years ...	53.9	52.0	52.5	50.5	49.1	47.0	50.2	48.1	49.87	47.96	51.2	50.4
$9\frac{1}{2}$ years ...	59.2	57.1	57.5	55.3	53.8	50.9	54.2	52.2	53.64	51.50	52.5	53.0
$10\frac{1}{2}$ years ...	65.3	62.4	62.4	60.6	59.5	56.4	59.6	58.6	59.81	57.37	60.0	58.8
$11\frac{1}{2}$ years ...	70.2	68.8	68.3	66.6	65.4	62.4	66.7	63.2	66.51	63.52	68.4	62.7
$12\frac{1}{2}$ years ...	76.9	78.3	73.9	74.3	70.9	68.8	72.0	69.7	71.00	69.94	70.8	70.0
$13\frac{1}{2}$ years ...	84.8	88.7	80.7	84.9	76.1	77.8	77.9	78.9	78.75	79.74	82.3	84.5
$14\frac{1}{2}$ years ...	94.9	98.4	89.1	93.3	84.9	88.0	89.4	90.7	86.13	87.66	88.0	92.0
$15\frac{1}{2}$ years ...	107.1	106.1	101.9	103.0	95.8	97.6	97.0	98.2	98.18	99.10	91.7	98.0
$16\frac{1}{2}$ years ...	121.0	112.0	113.8	110.9	109.0	105.9	108.1	108.9	112.2	105.0	110.0	104.0
$17\frac{1}{2}$ years ...	127.5	115.5	122.8	116.0	122.1	110.6	121.6	109.8	123.6	109.0	127.0	113.0
$18\frac{1}{2}$ years ...	132.6	115.2	......	115.5	130.4	113.3	131.7	117.7	132.9	115.0	130.0	113.7
$19\frac{1}{2}$ years ...	......	......	......	115.1	137.8	112.5	137.7	118.3	133.2	120.0	......	......
$20\frac{1}{2}$ years ...	......	......	......	118.8	......	......	......	......	142.6	118.3	......	......
$21\frac{1}{2}$ years ...	......	......	......	......	......	......	......	......	......	119.8	......	......

Age	Iowa. (Gilbert). About 50 of each sex for each age.		Pennsylvania. (Hall). 2,434 males (nude).		Sweden Commission. (Key). 15,000 boys, 3,000 girls.		Denmark Commission. (Hertel). 17,134 boys, 11,250 girls.		Moscow. (Erismann). 2,453 boys, 1,495 girls.		Turin. (Pagliani). 1,048 boys, 968 girls.	
	M.	F.	M.	F.	M.	F.	M.	F.	M.	F.	M.	F.
3½ years ...											27.3	24.7
4½ years ...											29.8	28.9
5½ years ...											33.5	33.1
6½ years ...	45.9	41.6			45.2		46.3	44.1	44.1	42.8	36.8	36.2
7½ years ...	51.4	47.4			50.3	47.6	49.6	47.4	48.5	47.0	42.8	39.0
8½ years ...	55.0	51.0			57.8	55.1	52.9	51.8	53.1	48.5	45.6	41.9
9½ years ...	61.6	58.1	58.4		64.6	59.3	57.3	56.2	61.1	56.4	49.4	48.3
10½ years ...	63.7	62.1	66.1		66.8	64.8	62.8	61.7	67.2	60.4	54.7	54.5
11½ years ...	72.4	69.2	71.7		71.0	70.3	68.3	67.2	73.4	66.8	58.6	59.3
12½ years ...	78.2	79.7	80.5		76.1	79.1	73.9	75.0	82.9	80.5	64.6	66.0
13½ years ...	90.9	94.1	89.7		82.9	87.3	80.5	83.8	91.5	89.3	72.8	76.1
14½ years ...	102.0	99.9	99.6		93.3	98.8	89.3	92.6	102.7	94.4	80.7	84.9
15½ years ...	117.0	111.3	108.7		103.2	107.8	102.6	102.6	116.8	99.9	92.2	96.6
16½ years ...	130.0	111.6	125.7		115.3	113.8	116.8	112.4	126.6	101.0	104.1	100.8
17½ years ...	140.1	121.0	133.8		127.0	120.4	126.8		132.5		116.2	104.7
18½ years ...	142.6	125.5	138.7		135.1	124.1	134.5				118.6	107.1
19½ years ...	145.5	126.4	140.7		139.6	126.6					121.3	
20½ years ...			142.6		143.7	127.2						
21½ years ...			145.1									

86 HEREDITY AND CHILD CULTURE

Rural Schools

A number of years ago, Dr. Thomas D. Wood of Teachers College, who has had a wide experience along educational lines, gave some interesting data as to the condition of children attending rural schools. He found that more than half the children in the United States are attending these country schools. In a carefully prepared table, which includes all parts of the country, it is shown that children attending these rural schools are less healthy and are handicapped by more physical defects than are the children of the cities, even including those living in the slums. Dr. Wood finds that more than twice as many country children as city children suffer from mal-nutrition; the former are also more anæmic, have more lung trouble, and include more mental defectives than do the latter. In a recent communication, he has stated that eye vision standards are very lax in rural schools. He declares that country children are not being given as careful cultivation as crops and live stock. He finds, moreover, that 21 per cent. of American children have eye defects, and such conditions may cause bright children to become dull.

Defective eyes with imperfect vision may

THE SCHOOL CHILD 87

cause blurring of sight, headache, dizziness, nervous irritation and lack of control. Dr. Wood believes that educational experts in this country are coming to an increased appreciation of the importance of the eye in school work.

A concerted effort to improve the health and normal development of school children should be made by parents, teachers, and physical directors. As a start, more time in the school curriculum could be given to a careful study of the physical condition of the pupils. This should be done by physicians accustomed to such work and not by mere physical trainers. The latter are not capable of recognizing abnormal conditions of the heart, lungs or other internal organs, yet much may depend on such knowledge.

Correct Posture

One of the fundamental requirements is the teaching of correct posture, both standing and sitting. This will not only redound to future health but add to the personal appearance of the individual. A correct poise can be attained by a little practice at this time which will last all through life.

The chest should be carried high and arched

88 HEREDITY AND CHILD CULTURE

forward, with shoulders held squarely back, the neck straight, the chin pointed in, and the abdomen also held firmly in. Such a carriage, accompanied by deep, full breathing will make both for health and grace. The muscles of the back and abdomen can thus be strengthened and an improved tone imparted to the whole system. An indirect but appreciable help can also be rendered to some common ailments, of which indigestion and constipation are perhaps the commonest. Boys and girls, soon to become young men and women, no matter how plain of feature they may be, can become attractive to look upon by being taught always to hold themselves erect and in the proper posture. There is a great contrast between an attractive physical poise and the slouchy position so often seen in boys and girls, especially the latter. The débutante stoop now affected by many young women is distressing to view.

School Equipment

The tendency of many school children to faulty posture may be due to desks or chairs not being of proper size or shape. There may thus ensue an undue curving of the back with a contraction of the chest. The desk may be

THE SCHOOL CHILD 89

too high or too low, and the chair is often placed too far back from the desk. The seat for each child should be of the same height as the length of the leg from the knee to the foot, so that when sitting the sole and heel can rest easily on the floor. If the seat is too low the body is bowed forward, and if too high only the toes touch the floor and a strain is thus put on the whole body. When the desk is too high the spinal column, which is very supple in the young, in thrown into a condition of lateral curvature. When many hours each day are spent in unnatural or constricted positions, the result cannot fail to be disastrous. The room, as well as its appliances, should be conducive to health, as such a large portion of every child's life is spent in school. Ventilation and light are of great importance. Cross ventilation from windows open at the top is usually the most satisfactory.

Each child should be allowed about twenty square feet of floor space and at least two hundred and fifty to three hundred cubic feet of air space. Of course, even these allowances will be insufficient unless there is a free supply of pure air. The windows should be placed as high as possible toward the ceiling for good light as well as ventilation. A northern light

90 HEREDITY AND CHILD CULTURE

is preferable, but from whatever direction it comes, it should strike the book of the pupil from behind, and, if possible, from the left. Glaring sunlight is hard on the eyes, and any dazzling light may be avoided by window shades made of some kind of gray material. The walls of the room are best tinted with a shade of gray, and every part should be well lighted. The best temperature of the room during winter would be about 68° F.

Physicians and sanitarians should oftener be placed on school boards in order to superintend health conditions and see that they are right.

Intellectual effort and hours of confinement should be carefully gauged according to the age of the child. Some years ago the hours of work and sleep required during childhood and youth were tabulated by the Royal Sanitary Institute of Great Britain as follows :

Age of pupils	Hours of work per day	Hours of sleep per night
From 5 to 6 years	1	13½
,, 6 to 7 ,,	1½	13
,, 7 to 8 ,,	2	12½
,, 8 to 9 ,,	2½	12
,, 9 to 10 ,,	3	11½
,, 10 to 12 ,,	3	11
,, 12 to 14 ,,	5	10½
,, 14 to 16 ,,	6	10
,, 16 to 18 ,,	7	9½
,, 18 to 19 ,,	8	9

It should be remembered that little children

THE SCHOOL CHILD 91

easily tire on mental exertion, which should not be continued too long without interruption. The table given will serve as a guide in this respect for the early years.

Athletics

Plenty of out-door exercise is required by the growing child and youth in order to lay up a store of vigour for future use. While a certain amount of indoor gymnasium exercise may be valuable, nothing is so beneficial to the boy or girl as play in the open air. In certain lines, however, there may be danger of carrying exercise too far, especially during the period of adolescence. This is shown in the craze for athletics seen in many schools and colleges. The outcome of this excessive interest is a few over-developed athletes and a majority of students barred out entirely owing to the high physical standard required for great competitive contests. School and college athletics, as at present conducted, usually conserve and over-develop the strong and eliminate the weak, just the ones needing most attention.

It is questionable whether eventually more physical harm than good does not come even to the athletes themselves. The terrific strain

92 HEREDITY AND CHILD CULTURE

put upon the vital organs, especially the heart and lungs, involved in these close competitive struggles, is sometimes followed by lasting ill effects. The excessive development of the muscular system in a person who is shortly to settle down to sedentary pursuits may end in disastrous results. The blood that should nourish the vital organs is appropiated in the building up of powerful and useless muscles which may result in a loss to the general vitality. The proper functioning of what may be called the great vegetative organs, such as the heart, lungs, and the liver are the important pre-requisites to health and long life, and not enormous muscles which are not put to constant use. A system of physical training that devotes excessive attention to the few and hence cannot give a careful study to the necessary all-round development of the many, is not a proper system and does not make for general and widely diffused health and vigour among the young.

Adolescence

During the latter part of school life there is ushered in a most interesting period of physical and mental activity,—adolescence. This is the time of life that intervenes between the beginning of puberty and the full development of the

THE SCHOOL CHILD 93

bodily frame. In the male, this may occupy the years from 14 to 25, and in the female from 12 to 21. In the early part of this period there is very marked nutritive activity which usually lessens during the latter part of the interval.

Up to the beginning of this time the child has lived the life of the race, but now he begins to develop his own individual life, and family traits come out more strongly. There is a rapid growth of the body, especially marked in certain internal structures, such as the bones, heart and lungs and reproductive organs, with increase in blood pressure and in general glandular activity.

As growth and development are rapid during adolescence, nothing must be allowed to conflict with the physical nature at this time. Overstrain in school must be guarded against. It is especially desirable that girls shall not be pushed in their studies at the beginning of adolescence. At a time when a new and most important life function is being established, the nervous energy and blood should not be diverted to the brain, as they can be better utilized in other parts of the body to the lasting health of the child. It must be borne in mind that infancy and adolescence are the two most rapidly

94 HEREDITY AND CHILD CULTURE

formative epochs of life, and quick growth predisposes to all kinds of disturbances.

At this period the peculiarities of sex begin to manifest themselves, and boys and girls cease to mingle in the indiscriminate way of early childhood. Up to twelve years there need not be much differentiation of the sexes, but after this they must be separately considered.

The boys are apt to show self-assurance, conceit, and many other evidences of egoism; the girls tend more to idealizing and romantic imaginings. Vague aspirations and a general restlessness show the stirring of a new life in the child's mind. Ideals begin to take strong hold, and, although often crude, prophesy in a general way the future bent of the character. If any trait is entirely absent at this time, it is not apt to be seen later in life.

There is no period of life when careful and sympathetic oversight and training are of such importance. The emotional nature now becomes active, with varying phases and manifestations. Religious and moral questions may assume importance, and it is the age of conversion.

Parents should study and guide these nascent emotions so that they will assume a normal and healthy form. This is especially im

THE SCHOOL CHILD 95

when the child tends to be morbid and intro-
spective. A careful moral training is as important as that directed toward the physical and
mental natures. It is especially important to
teach the child that there is a difference between real and imaginary conditions. An effort
should be made to convert introspection into
activity and at the same time to give some
insight into the realities of life. This will be
an aid in counteracting selfishness as well as
in true character building. The imagination
becomes very active at this time and care must
be taken that it is fed with wholesome reading
and environment.

CHAPTER IX

MENTAL CULTURE

IN the first chapter attention has been called to the fact that in the human race evolution is now confined to the brain. In the modern struggle for existence, men fight with their brains and not with the muscles. At birth, the brain although fairly large, is undeveloped and watery, especially in the higher areas.

The lower portion of the brain, the eventual seat of the subconscious mind, is quickly acted on by all sorts of physical and mental stimuli. The larger muscular actions, such as movements of the arms and legs, are exhibited from the time of birth, but the smaller muscles with their finer action, shown by the co-ordination of the fingers and picking up objects, are regulated by brain centres that are on a little higher level. The structure of the brain and the controlling forces are gradually developed from below upward. The upper brain comes gradually into play as a result of stimuli and education, and the functions of the mind begin to un-

MENTAL CULTURE 97

fold. The convoluted surface of the upper brain regulates the functions of control and inhibition which are the latest products of evolution. These later functions are therefore more unstable than the lower and more automatic reflexes, and constant training and education are accordingly required. This higher brain machinery, with the deep convolutions arranged in functional groups, is what makes education produce results and also opens up the widest possibilities. The effective use of the brain calls for the best training in order to reach the highest development possible for each individual.

The motor areas of the spinal chord are quite highly developed at this time, but the sensory portion is not functionally active. This explains many of the nervous phenomena of beginning life. The higher cerebral centres exercise a feeble inhibition over the lower and more active motor centres of the spinal cord. Hence what would be a sensory phenomenon in later life is a motor one in the young infant. The best example of this is seen in the way certain illnesses begin. What is a sensory symptom in the adult—a chill—is reflected into a motor arc and becomes a convulsion in the infant. In its nervous mechanism, the new-

98 HEREDITY AND CHILD CULTURE

born baby is not unlike a fully-developed frog. Pain is not active at this time, and while doubtless conscious of unpleasant sensations, the young baby does not experience pain in the ordinary sense. A baby born without any brain will automatically cry. By the end of the first year, crying may ensue from a real feeling of pain.

Just after birth the brain and nerve centres act only automatically, or by reflex action. Touch and taste are present at birth, but the baby is deaf for the first few days and will not follow an object with its eyes until the third week. The eyes should never be exposed to bright lights. By the third month, the baby reaches out its arms for objects and may recognize individuals. The rudiments of memory are now developed, and by the fourth or fifth month a few persons may be remembered and recognized. It is not until the third year, however, that memory develops very rapidly. Efforts at speaking usually begin at the end of the first year when single words may be uttered. At the close of the second year short sentences are attempted.

By the third year there begins to be the ability to draw an inference and slight powers of reasoning develop. Here is where education

MENTAL CULTURE 99

should begin to have an effect, always remembering that while the little child's preceptions and emotions are active, there is not much volitional power or self-control. The child should be taught to use its senses and muscles before trying to cultivate memory or imagination. Precocious children should not be pushed forward ; they have usually over-nervous temperaments, Sometimes bright children by being thrown too exclusively into the society of adults become precocious. They like to show off by exhibiting feats of memory or special aptitudes, as in music or dancing. Their exaggerated perceptions soon disappear and they later, often develop into very commonplace personalities. This is apt to be true as a rule, although many real geniuses have early developed precocity. It is a safe rule, however, that this tendency should not be encouraged. Children who are self-conscious and always eager to occupy the centre of the stage need repression.

In the early years, imitation and suggestion play leading parts, At the end of infancy and during early childhood, the imitative faculties come specially into play. The acts of older children, of adults, and even of animals, are faithfully copied without much idea of their

100 HEREDITY AND CHILD CULTURE

significance. Up to the age of seven years, much of the training and education of the child must come from imitation. He learns by imitating, and little escapes his watchful eye. This throws a great responsibility upon parents and teachers, as a defective environment is at once reflected by an observing and imitative little child. Up to the age of seven, most of the playing of children is imitative, shown by the delight in dolls and numerous toys representing objects in real life ; but after this, especially in boys, games take on a more competitive form, involving muscular exercise.

The little child being so imitative, suggestion plays a very important part in training. The absence of the critical faculty at this time leaves the field open for suggestion to work with great force. Hence in training the little child, suggestion must be largely employed, as the imitative faculty allows it to work to great advantage.

It must be remembered that the child exhibits the elemental human forces and instincts. Just as the emotions are developed in the race before the reason, so it is with children. They can be moved by their sympathies long before they can be influenced by their intellect. Love is a surer guide for them than reason. This is the

MENTAL CULTURE 101

secret of the success of many mothers and of a few teachers. The latter however, are too apt to try to cultivate the intellect before the emotions and feelings are considered, and hence they often make a failure of both.

Education

The importance of proper education is stressed by the fact that the early impressions of the young are never entirely forgotten. Few realize the power of ideas, especially when early implanted. The effect of ideas when reinforced by strong suggestion has an especially quick result upon the plastic mind of the child. It took only about two generations of careful instruction in State Schools to cause the obsession of the superman and world dominion to take hold of youthful Germany, and she sprang at the throat of the world, although the older generation was naturally friendly and law abiding. The Jesuit is usually satisfied if he can control the early years.

Attention has been directed to the fact that little children cannot concentrate attention very long on one subject, so that mental exercises should be short with frequent intercurrent rests. As a rule, it is better for a child to be with others, as work, study and play with

102 HEREDITY AND CHILD CULTURE

school-mates is more favourable than being too much alone or too exclusively with adults.

At the beginning of mental training there is more of a tendency to do too much rather than too little. One must first be sure that all the senses can function properly from the possession of sound organs. They must all be properly co-ordinated,—touch, taste, smell, sight and hearing. As touch and muscle sense are earliest developed, the manual part of training is important, and education first functions along this line. The optic nerve is about eight times larger than the auditory nerve, and it is certainly eight times easier to teach by sight than by hearing. But while the eye is the best channel for information, care must be taken that there is no over-strain. We must always remember that what is observed by the eye is registered in the brain. Little children are often allowed to see too much. All kinds of exciting pictures are presented at the movies, including warfare, scenes in foreign lands and strange experiences of all kinds. These are all projected on the sensitive brain of the child, and too early forcing may mean a later reaction in which the child pays up for impressions that are crowded too soon upon an immature mind.

MENTAL CULTURE 103

In a recent report upon the activities of six of Chicago's high schools, it was stated after a questionnaire that 87 per cent. of 3000 children attended the movies from one to seven times a week. The abnormal character of many of the pictures, including gunmen, criminals, sexual problems and all kinds of exciting scenes, cannot but have a disastrous effect upon the young and inexperienced mind. Properly censored, however, the movie has great educational as well as amusement possibilities.

The child should early be taught to think,—even in a rudimentary way,—and to think straight. One of the causes of the confusion of the time is that so few persons really think. They have not been taught this important function early enough,—they think loosely and talk loosely. As so many absorbed in the routine of daily life do not seem to have the time or ability to think a subject through, a small number are permitted to do the thinking for all, frequently with disastrous effect. Let us start a saner generation by training the opening minds to accustom themselves to thought. The thoughtlessness that starts early, too often lasts through life.

While true education must be a life undertaking, it is in the proper training of the young

104 HEREDITY AND CHILD CULTURE

that this question assumes its greatest importance. Health and growth must both be considered at this time, but, as the period is a short one, the tendency is toward over-pressure and a hurried undertaking of many things. This is a great evil, but much of it might be avoided if teachers and parents had a truer conception of the real function of education.

The tendency is to confuse education with mere instruction. The object of the former is training, that of the latter information. The object of education is not primarily or solely to impart knowledge ; it is, rather so to train the mind that it will have the capacity for selection and development and can thus put itself in proper adjustment with the larger and higher life of the race.

The object of instruction, on the other hand, is to store the mind with useful and interesting facts. In the case of children there is apt to be too much instruction and too little education. The pressure that tries to induce extensive knowledge is in danger of lessening vitality without giving corresponding power, success or happiness. Too many studies are usually given to children, and this crowding creates a serious problem. Not only is depth sacrificed to extent of surface in this form of mental

MENTAL CULTURE 105

training, but too little time is left for physical exercise and amusement.

The growth of forced and so-called higher education has been relatively more rapid with girls than with boys. In the former, the question is complicated by the importance to themselves and the race of proper physical and sexual development during the period of growth. At the time of maturing, the body is more important than the mind, yet this is just the time that the girl is pushed hardest in her educational career if she expects to pursue a course in high school or college. The women's colleges are increasing in number and importance and have set the educational pace, as in the case with the men's colleges. While no one of intelligence questions the desirability of a good education for girls,—whether the kind of training they get in their colleges is the best still forms an open question. The aims seem to be to put the girls through the same educational hopper as the boys, irrespective of their physical and mental differences. The feminine mind differs from the masculine mind, just as the feminine body differs from the masculine body and both, to a certain extent, require specialized training. These differences have deep-seated biological causes that must not be overlooked in

106 HEREDITY AND CHILD CULTURE

education. The fundamental differences in the physio-psychological make-up of the sexes must early be considered. It would seem as if the higher education of young women might properly place emphasis on such subjects as modern languages, literature, music, hygiene,—both personal and domestic,—the selection and chemistry of foods, the care and training of children, the theory and practice of modern charity and cognate subjects, together with a careful physical development. In a word, she should be educated with the idea of becoming a wife rather than a school-teacher. The keenness of girls for higher education is shown by the fact that they are beginning to outnumber the men in colleges on a co-educational basis, and the girls show a general preponderance in numbers over the boys in the high schools of New York, Philadelphia and Chicago. In both sexes there is needed a simplification of the whole educational process.

One detail of school life that might be corrected is the needless prolonging of vacations, which tends to make the working time too short and strenuous. It would be better for health to restrict the length of vacations and to work under less pressure during the rest of the year. Some reorganization of modern education at all

MENTAL CULTURE 107

ages, but especially in the early years, is much to be desired, and educators should face this problem. It must primarily be borne in mind that a true education of the young should be based upon knowledge of biographical, physiological and psychological processes and carried on in conformity to them.

Professor G. Stanley Hall has approached the question in the following words, [1]—"We are progressively forgetting that for the complete apprenticeship to life, youth needs repose, leisure, art, legends, romance, idealization, and in a word humanism, if it is to enter the kingdom of man well equipped for man's highest work in the world. In education our very kindergartens, which outnumber those of any other land, by dogma and hypersophistication tend to exterminate the naiveté that is the glory of childhood. Everywhere the mechanical and formal triumph over content and substance, the letter over the spirit, the intellect over morals, lesson setting and hearing over real teaching, technical over the essential, information over education, marks over edification, and method over matter."

We must always remember that the time for education is short. According to some

[1] *Adolescence*, D. Appleton & Co.

108 HEREDITY AND CHILD CULTURE

psychologists, it is a serious fact that mental plasticity largely ceases with youth. The mind is apt to be closed to new ideals after the early years. While this may be an exaggeration in some cases, it is nevertheless true in a majority of instances, and stresses the great importance of a right management of mental training. This means that correct methods and ideals must form the groundwork for a structure of efficiency and high development.

CHAPTER X

MORAL CULTURE

THE mental and moral natures in their development are closly allied. The conduct of the child is largely influenced by the tone and temper of those about him. If a proper poise and self-control exists, it is sure to be reflected in the children. A cultivated home will do more for the child's mental and moral health than the formal education of the finest schools.

In a study of the moral nature of the child, we must sharply distinguish the essential from the non-essential in character building. Thus a sort of rowdyism due to an excess of animal spirits need not be constantly repressed, but any duplicity must be instantly noticed and reprimanded. The gravity of the latter, however, depends on the age. Professor Barnes has truly said that a lie from a three-year old is normal ; from a six-year old, unimportant ; from a nine-year old, serious ; from a twelve-year old, tragic.

If a point is once made, it must be carried out,

110 HEREDITY AND CHILD CULTURE

no matter how much of a struggle is required, and it is therefore wise to make an issue as rarely as possible, and then only for really essential points. The character of many a child is injured by querulous rebukes, constantly administered, until he becomes to be considered as a sort of outlaw, all perhaps for small offences that involve no essential moral question. A little judicial blindness and an occasional kindly talk, combined with efforts to gain the confidence and interest of the child, and guide his exuberant energy in proper directions will do much to conserve his moral and social self-respect. There is sometimes danger of too much as well as too little discipline. We must be careful never to break the spirit of the child. There are only a few imported dogmas that always must be authoritatively enforced.

There exists in many children a touch of barbarism that is merely an evidence of underdevelopment. Lombroso goes so far as to trace certain analogies between the child and the criminal. He considers that the germs of criminality are met with, not by exception, but normally in the early years of human life. As in the embryo, there occur naturally certain forms that will be monstrosities in the adult, so the child represents a man of undeveloped moral

MORAL CULTURE 111

strength. Lombroso places passion and vengefulness, vanity and cruelty in this comparison between the child and the criminal. The great criminologist certainly goes too far in exaggerating this analogy, but it may afford food for serious thought and observation to those who study and bring up children. Apparent cruelty, shown in a callousness to suffering, is often seen in children, but is due more to ignorance and lack of experience as to the meaning of pain than to defective moral sensibility.

The phenomenon of sex should be explained to children as soon as they are old enough to understand. By treating this subject in a matter-of-fact way, and stripping it of the unwholesome mystery so often surrounding the facts, the child can readily comprehend all that it is necessary to know. Parents are the proper ones to give this knowledge and they can prepare themselves to impart it without much trouble. They may start with explaining the reproduction of new life in the vegetable world and thence lead up to animals and man. It can take its place in connection with general nature-study which is always profitable and desirable for the child. All manifestations of life on the physical side must be presented in a normal manner, so that nothing unclean may be

112 HEREDITY AND CHILD CULTURE

suggested. The handling of the sex organs, except for cleanliness, can be brought in here in a natural manner and linked up with general hygiene. In this way one can avoid a suggestion that might prove undesirable. Children often know more on these subjects than their parents think, although in a distorted, unwholesome form. Their views must be clarified, and, at the same time, they can be taught the bad results of evil habits. Most children wish to be strong and excel in sports, and an appeal can be made from this angle to avoid whatever will lessen health and vigour.

Much of our physical, mental, and even moral health depends on the proper functioning of the endocrine glands,—sometimes known as the glands of internal secretion. Many of the chemical reactions so necessary to bodily health are produced or controlled by these glands. The thyroids, adrenals, pituitary bodies and other similar glands produce hormones (messengers) that are carried by the blood-stream to all parts of the body and produce marked physical and mental effects. Some biologists believe that the endocrines have a large influence upon the heredity and development of man. It is known that certain forms of feeble-mindedness are produced by a lack of

MORAL CULTURE 113

some internal secretion, and in one variety,—
the Cretin,—by giving thyroid by mouth, the
body and mind are both re-invigorated. Some
even believe that certain criminals are really
gland-victims. On the other hand, strong
emotion will quickly affect these secretions.
Sudden fear will have a marked effect upon the
thyroid and adrenal glands, and courage, as
shown in the excitement of battle, calls forth
the secretion of the adrenals. There is a constant chemical re-adjustment going on in the
body by the interaction of these various glands ;
not only mental conditions, but the very
architecture of the body is largely influenced by
them. Thus both giants and dwarfs are largely
developed by the irregular action of the pituitary
gland. Like other phenomena of life, the harmon-
ious action of these mysterious and powerful
glands are best-set in motion by healthy growth
at the beginning. The early development of
self-control will have beneficial effects all
through life on these important glands.

With reference to actual delinquency, childhood traits must be early watched, and corrective
measures at once applied to all moral lapses.
It is believed that criminals are always made
before the age of twenty-one. They must
therefore be caught and reformed early if at

H

114 HEREDITY AND CHILD CULTURE

all. Many years ago, Dr. Ales Hrdlicka, the anthropologist, at my request made a careful examination of 1000 inmates of the New York Juvenile Asylum. These children were committed to the asylum by the court for petty crimes or gross neglect on the part of the parents. In his conclusions, he stated that when the children were admitted to the institution, they were almost invariably in some way, both morally and physically, inferior to healthy children from good social classes at large. A closer observation, however, revealed the fact that the inferiorities of the children who became inmates of the Juvenile Asylum were in the majority of cases only the results of neglect, or of improper nutrition, or of both these causes combined. Many of the children were more or less neglected, or spoiled, or less developed or stronger than they should be ; but a really inferior child, that is, an inherently vicious, or an imbecile child, or a child who could not be much improved by better food and better hygienic surroundings, was a very rare exception.

This constitutes a striking demonstration of the effect of early neglect and the possibilities of regeneration.

The best way to eliminate evil is to stress

MORAL CULTURE 115

the good in every individual. By filling life with activities that enlist the interest of the child there will be neither time nor opportunity for the lower traits to develop. Let their energies be directed toward a constructive and creative outlet.

Some children have to be taught to play, as they seem lacking in initiative in this direction ; organized play may have a favourable mental and moral effect. Let us start right in this direction as the habit of happiness may then continue into after life. It may well be that vigourous play in the growing years can have an influence on the prolongation of life and the prevention of degenerative diseases ; also to raise the question as to whether our unsatisfactory organization of leisure life, through which people get no real self-expression, may not have something to do with the wide extent of functional nervous disorders.

Children of the well-to-do should early be taught to sympathize with misfortune and extend aid where possible. Even a small knowledge of the hard life conditions that surround so many people will tend to eliminate the innate selfishness that is so common among our better-favoured youth. A cultivation of the moral nature should be started early and con-

116 HEREDITY AND CHILD CULTURE

tinued all through the developing period. Th e child can soon recognize the difference between right and wrong, and this vital distinction must be both taught and enforced.

Finally, a careful religious training, when freed from obsolete dogmas, will be most helpful in developing the best character attainable. A simple, rational faith in the moral order of the world and in a Supreme Being who is working by the laws of nature and life for the ultimate good of the race can early be inculcated. This will start a sense of responsibility that will develop with later years.

It is unfortunate that the spiritual life of children should be so often neglected by parents and teachers. As a result, too often we are raising a lot of lusty young pagans who, as they grow up, like Gallio, will "care for none of these things." No one quicker than the child reacts to the widespread materialism of the day. It is a strange fact that while materialism is growing stronger as a social force, it is losing ground as an interpretation of life to the thinking classes. Here is a chance for the coming generation to be given a truer orientation of life than commonly exists at present. It is wise to start early in teaching the eternal verities, and the simpler the faith the easier it will be to inculcate.

MORAL CULTURE 117

The so-called ages of faith have passed, never to return. We need not unduly grieve over this since they were likewise ages of ignorance and superstition. Yet never has the necessity of strong and simple belief been greater than at present. Careful observers of life cannot help noticing that as faith lessens, actual living is apt to weaken and degenerate. This rule is true in spite of the few apparent exceptions where a heredity of strong character steadies a life that has lost belief. Religion best furnishes what psychologists might call the *sustaining motive* to right actions and a correct life. Only a few fundamental religious truths are really necessary to nourish the higher life. Let them be carefully implanted in the opening mind rather than trying to teach doctrines that were evidently developed largely out of social conditions existing when they were formulated. The danger of unreal beliefs being early taught is that, with the age of intellectual awakening, the true as well as the false in religion may be thrown aside.

The little child will be the ultimate judge of the world, before his problems and questionings most plans of philosophy, codes of ethics and systems of theology somehow prove stumbling, inadequate and unworkable.

118 HEREDITY AND CHILD CULTURE

The age needs a great voice that will find a way between the gnostic and the agnostic in developing the religious and spiritual life of the future. Perhaps some child of the present day will later furnish this voice.

CHAPTER XI

NERVE CULTURE

WE seem to have struck an era of "nerves." Large numbers of men and women show a nervous instability that often has its roots in defective training and example during the opening years. Early education and control are necessary to check this growing tendency.

Probably more trouble is produced in the world by neurotics than by criminals. The former do not react in a normal and healthy manner to the stimuli of their environment and are easily maladjusted in all their relationships. These persons drift from neurologist to quack, from astrologer to osteopath, and usually end in one of the happiness cults whose followers spend their time in joyously dodging obligations and realities. Numerous imaginary diseases are constantly encountered and cured by imaginary remedies. Not a few obscure illnesses are really due to what the psychologists call a defence reaction in men and women, especially the latter, who fail to adjust them-

120 HEREDITY AND CHILD CULTURE

selves to their surroundings. They have an inner feeling of inadequacy and unconsciously fall back on some functional and obscure nervous trouble as a way of escape. The only thing that will really and permanently help these neurotics,—re-education—is overlooked. Perhaps it is too hard and honest for trial.

It is much more hopeful to try to check this tendency at the beginning by proper education. The earliest years are the impressionable ones ; intellectual and emotional instability can get a good start at this time. While it is generally thought that heredity is responsible for nervous instability, I believe the condition is oftener due to faulty environment during the early years. According to Freud, the neurotic is manufactured before the age of six years.

Modern psychology has explained, to a certain extent, how these phenomena arise. What are known as complexes may consist of certain groups of co-ordinated motions called into play by various actions, as in violin playing ; again, they may comprise groups of ideas or emotions. By constant repetition, these motor or psychic groupings become fixed into habit. It is in the subconscious mind that complexes oftenest remain, as it were, concealed until brought into play. A complex

NERVE CULTURE 121

may not exist in the conscious mind at all; it may oftener be in the subconscious mind, only waiting for certain experiences or influences to bring it forth. These connected ideas are often joined with emotional conditions that have a marked effect on action or conduct. The whole character may often be influenced by combinations of complexes.

A large number of subconscious ideas and complexes are acquired during the first years of life. They may form the roots of obscure ailments that will be carried on into later years. Thus neurotics are made by conditions that usually have their origin in childhood, forming compulsions and inhibitions that trail along through after-life. It is not necessary to believe with the Freudians that there is always a sexual genesis of disturbing complexes, although this element is doubtless frequently present. Strong impressions or emotions of any kind may have a lasting effect. Suppressions and repressions are too frequently employed and may result in an imbalance of character. Undesirable trends in infancy and childhood may land an adult in an unenviable mental condition. Dr. Spaulding states that too great attention cannot be given to such factors, particularly in the first five years of life,

122 HEREDITY AND CHILD CULTURE

since it is being recognised more and more that it is in the earliest years that the great tragedies occur that tend to warp seriously the individual expression of energy of later years.

Grief, fear, worry, anger, apprehension and emotional shocks may become fixed and form the early beginnings of what will eventually lead to individual and social maladjustments. We must be especially careful not to implant fear in the developing mind of the young. The nervous child is especially liable to become malajusted in the emotional field. Although many disturbing experiences in the young child's mental and moral life may be long forgotten, their effects are held in the subconscious mind, and it may be years before a submerged emotion finds outlet in an indirect or surprising manifestation. An emotion or feeling suppressed in one way may find "sublimation," according to the psychologists, in an entirely different direction.

All this emphasizes the importance of early training. It is much better and easier to try to form good habits than reform bad ones.

Fathers and mothers with unstable character and flighty moods will find their children developing the same characteristics from imitation. Fussy, neurotic parents must realise their re-

NERVE CULTURE 123

sponsibility and try to control their nervous instability for the sake of their children if not for themselves. Children must be guarded, as far as possible, from severe emotional shocks. Their lives must be made as happy as circumstances will permit. The play instinct should always be developed. It must be remembered that apparent egoism or intense shyness may be only manifestations of defence reactions. The child must be encouraged in developing his natural qualities, and efforts should be made to bring out the best in him. Perhaps the mother can most satisfactorily control the emotions and direct the will, and the father see that self-reliance be cultivated. A normal, happy family life will best fit the child to make proper adjustments to the varying environment of later years. Finally, the child cannot too early be taught to face reality and learn to appreciate the fact that life is a process of adjustment.

CHAPTER XII

THE IMPORTANCE OF PROPER NUTRITION

THE great importance of good nutrition during the developmental years cannot be over-estimated. At this time the structure of the body, including the most vital tissues, is being built up and the organism thus formed must serve for the whole of life. If proper growth does not take place during the period of natural development, no later compensation is possible.

At this time, a double function of nutrition is required, first, that of growth, and second that of maintainance or keeping the body in operation. By the latter is meant a supply of energy and heat, and as the child by its growth and activity burns up more fuel than the adult, it is doubly important to supply a sufficiency of proper food to serve as fuel. Hence, at this time a carefully balanced diet is very essential.

The great variety of articles in use as food all contain only a few essential principles— proteins, mineral matter, fats, carbohydrates

PROPER NUTRITION 125

and water, the latter constituting a large proportion of all foods. These different substances when taken into the body have various functions to perform. The proteins and mineral matter are used in the growth and repair of the body; the fats supply heat and energy and are deposited in the tissues for form and contour; the carbohydrates also supply heat and energy, and may be changed into fat in the system; the water gives bulk and solvent properties to the various tissues.

These food principles are found in a variety of forms and combinations. Protein exists as lean meat, the curd of milk, fish, poultry, eggs, cheese, beans, barley, oatmeal and the gluten of flour. The mineral matter consists largely of earthy salts, such as phosphate of lime and compounds of magnesium, sodium, potassium and iron. These substances are usually taken into the body in combination with the proteins. The fats are seen incorporated with meats, or as lard, butter, the cream of milk and vegetable oils. Carbohydrates are the various starches and sugars that are combined in cereals, potatoes, flour and vegetables.

It has recently been found that growth takes place not only from the chemical ingredients of foods but from mysterious substances known as

126 HEREDITY AND CHILD CULTURE

vitamines. If these substances are absent from foods, growth and nutrition will fail and certain deficiency diseases, such as rickets or scurvy will result. Although these living entities may be present only in most minute traces, they are necessary factors in nutrition if health is to be preserved. Thus no diet should be continued that does not contain one or more of the foods producing vitamines. The several varieties and the foods containing them have been divided into three classes—(A.) Vitamines soluble in fat, included in butter, eggs, cod liver oil, fat fish, lean meat, lettuce, spinach, fresh carrots, cabbage, and the germ of cereals ; (B.) Vitamines soluble in water, included in milk, eggs, lean meat, liver and various other glands, potatoes, cabbage, carrots, lettuce, turnips, nuts, wheat bran, the germ of cereals, apples, oranges, lemons, grapes, tomatoes, yeast ; (C.) Vitamines that prevent scurvy, also soluble in water, included in lean meat, liver, beef juice, cows' milk, cabbage, tomatoes, turnips, cresses, lettuce, apples, oranges, fresh lime juice, lemon juice, raspberries. Vitamine (A) is not much affected by heat, vitamine (B) should not be subjected to heat above the boiling point of water, and vitamine (C) is destroyed by heat and alkalies. For this reason, when

PROPER NUTRITION

all the milk given to infants and little children is preserved by heat, some fruit juice should be added to the dietary. It is always desirable to preserve the water in which vegetables are cooked so that the vitamines may be retained,

The vitamine problem is naturally more important during the growing period than later in life, as proper development cannot take place in their absence. A mixed diet containing a variety of the above-mentioned foods will always insure a sufficient supply, and it is hence not necessary to rely on any of the numerous proprietary preparations now flooding the market.

Milk is the universal food of all young mammals. It is the only food in nature that is complete in itself; it contains all the necessary elements for growth as well as those required for heat and energy production in a most digestible and absorbable form. While every species of mammalian young is perfectly nourished by the milk of its own mother, the food elements are present in varying proportions in different species, this depending largely on the rapidity of growth of the offspring; hence milks of one species require some alteration before being given to the young of another species.

128 HEREDITY AND CHILD CULTURE

In addition to nutrition, milk has properties which no other food possesses. It is fluid when secreted, but when taken into the body it is changed from a liquid into a semi-solid substance under the action of the secretions of the stomach. This seems to have the function of training the growing stomach to utilize solid food when it is more fully developed. This is due to a process of coagulation that takes place in one of the ingredients—the protein—which always alters the form of the milk when taken into the stomach. While a certain amount of protein is present in the milks of all animals and is necessary for tissue building and growth, this protein must not only be coagulable but must curd in a certain specific way in each species of animal, for the proper evolution of different digestive tracts. As nutrition is the basis of all physical life, we see how important a function milk performs at the very beginning of existence in developing and preparing the digestive tract for the digestion and assimilation of food that must nourish it in later life. Some years ago I brought out this fact, that milk, through its protein has a developmental as well as a nutritive function to perform.[1] The higher mortality following bottle feeding

[1] *The Scientific Monthly*, January, 1916.

PROPER NUTRITION 129

is not the only reason in favour of maternal nursing. In feeding the infant with milk from another species—the cow—we are putting a hard curdling milk into a stomach intended and adapted for soft, flocculent curds. This is the cause of much indigestion and such substitution fails to carry out one of the functions that milk was intended to perform in the scheme of evolution,—namely, in each species to specially develop certain parts of the gastro-intestinal tract that must later on perform most of the work of digestion.

Every effort should be made to have the mother nurse her infant, especially during the first months. If this were done there would not only be a distinct lowering of infant mortality but a more vigorous life would be insured. It is only necessary to note here that while the general infant mortality has been largely reduced, that occurring during the first month of life has not yet been lowered. Since milk is the only food that supplies all the ingredients required in the building up of bones, muscles and other tissues, and in the proportions and conditions required by each species, the natural milk is best supplied to the baby by its own mother. The important mineral ingredients, especially lime, so necessary in

I

130 HEREDITY AND CHILD CULTURE

bone building, are also most efficiently supplied by mother's milk.

The conservation of the milk of a healthy mother is of such great importance for the infant that every effort should be made to utilize it. We must first see that the breast is thoroughly emptied at each nursing, as this stimulates the secretion. If only a little milk is secreted, give what is there at each feeding and then at once supplement by the bottle. The regular use of the breast soon stimulates to better action. We must also furnish the mother with plenty of food that will supply materials best suited for making milk and which are rich in vitamines. The best source of the materials needed for making milk in the cow is the herbaceous plants. When the spring grass appears, cows produce the best milk and in the greatest quantities. These herbaceous plants are the original source of vitamines. They are also found in the germs or embryos of the grass seeds. The nursing mother should drink milk, also broths made from green leaves, such as spinach, lettuce, celery-tops, onion or beet-tops. A porridge or gruel made from cereals containing the germs will also be found of much value. Meat is desirable and should usually be taken twice daily. Sufficient rest should also be

134 HEREDITY AND CHILD CULTURE

A child should receive one food at least from the following groups every day :

1. Milk, and dishes made chiefly of milk (most important of the group as regards children's diet) ; meat, fish, poultry, eggs, and meat substitutes.
2. Bread and other cereal foods. Starchy vegetables, as potatoes.
3. Butter and other wholesome fats.
4. Green vegetables and fruits.
5. Simple sweets.

Calories as Measures of Food Values

The human body, like the automobile, is run as an internal combustion engine. Energy may be conveniently measured in terms of heat, the calorie or heat unit, being used for this purpose. A calorie is the quantity of heat required to raise the temperature of one litre of water one degree centigrade, or very nearly the amount of heat required to raise the temperature of one pound of water from 0° to 4° F. While all nutrients are possible sources of energy, the body should depend upon fats and carbohydrates as energy-producing foods, rather than upon protein, which has tissue building functions not possessed by the other nutrients. Moreover, fats are more efficient sources of energy than

PROPER NUTRITION 133

some focal infections that may affect distant parts of the body.

After considering the time and manner of eating, all that remains is to be sure that a properly balanced diet containing all the necessary ingredients for growth and development is given the child. The following is a convenient classification found in Farmers' Bulletin, No. 808 of the U.S. Government.

FOODS DEPENDED ON FOR MINERAL MATTERS, VEGETABLE ACIDS, AND BODY-REGULATING SUBSTANCES

Fruits :
  Apples, pears, etc.
  Bananas.
  Berries.
  Melons.
  Oranges, lemons, etc.

Vegetables :
  Salads—lettuce, celery, etc.
  Potherbs or "greens."
  Potatoes and root vegetables.
  Green peas, beans, etc.
  Tomatoes, squash, etc.

FOODS DEPENDED ON FOR PROTEIN

Milk, skim milk, cheese, etc.
Eggs.
Meat.
Poultry.

Fish.
Dried peas, beans, cowpeas, etc.
Nuts.

FOODS DEPENDED ON FOR STARCH

Cereal grains, meals, flours, etc.
Cereal breakfast foods.
Bread.
Crackers.

Macaroni and other pastes.
Cakes, cookies, starchy puddings, etc.
Potatoes and other starchy vegetables.

FOODS DEPENDED ON FOR SUGAR

Sugar.
Molasses.
Syrups.
Honey.

Candies.
Fruits preserved in sugar, jellies, and dried fruits.
Sweet cakes and desserts.

FOODS DEPENDED ON FOR FAT

Butter and cream.
Lard, suet, and other cooking fats.

Salt pork and bacon.
Table and salad oils.

132 HEREDITY AND CHILD CULTURE

games involving violent exercise, with a sandwich in one hand, from which hasty bites are taken during a lull in the game. The school day should be so arranged that a hot, nourishing dinner may be served during the noon hour. The heavy meal of the day should be given at this time to little children. Much of the malnutrition among school children is caused by faulty arrangement of meals due to prolonged or inconvenient school hours. Children should also early be taught to eat plain, wholesome food. Habits and tastes formed in the first years have much to do with food customs lasting all through life, and children should thus be taught to live on simple, nutritious and, if necessary, inexpensive foods. This should form part of their education. The palate must be educated as well as the brain.

The food given little children is often too soft. Hard, gritty substances are needed to exercise the teeth and develop the jaws. Too many sweets and sugary substances also affect the mouth as well as the digestive tract. These conditions favour early decay of the teeth, which does not occur among the lower animals. According to modern studies, the mouth assumes great importance in the economy of digestion and assimilation. It is likewise the source of

PROPER NUTRITION 181

enjoined; a restless, disturbed night will have a marked effect upon the secretion of mothers' milk. The importance of all this will be realized from the fact that over 80 per cent. of the babies dying before the completion of the first year are bottle-fed.

When cows' milk has to be entirely substituted, the greatest care in its collection and distribution must be exercised. An extra quality of cow's milk known as "certified milk" is now procurable in many communities and is preferable for babies. The exact formula and the method of diluting and preparing cow's milk for babies at different ages should be regulated by a skilful physician who can manage each case according to individual needs.

After the nursing period is over, the hours and methods of feeding are very important for good nutrition, as well as the selection of proper food. The value of eating slowly must early be stressed, as most children and many adults get in the habit of bolting their food. A few minutes rest before and after eating will do much to build up a vigorous digestion. During the school recess, lunch is often hastily bolted in order to have more time for engaging in play. Children may sometimes be seen in

PROPER NUTRITION 135

either protein or carbohydrates. It has been estimated that for every 100 calories, about 10 per cent. should be produced from proteins, 30 per cent. from fats, and 60 per cent. from carbohydrates. While foods yielding about 2,500 calories a day are required by average adults in sedentary pursuits, growing children may require 3,000 to 4,000 calories, or even more, during adolescence.

It is not wise, however, to put too much emphasis on calories in measuring nutritional needs. Heat measurement alone is not always a safe guide for the calculation of food values. This is especially true at the beginning of life when growth is the all important factor. The foods that *build* rather than those that readily undergo oxidation must be properly gauged if we are to have healthy development. This means that the great protein suppliers,—meat, eggs, fish, milk and cereals,—must have an important place in the dietary. An ounce of lean meat, furnishing 34 calories, contains 6.4 grams of protein ; an ounce of hominy, furnishing 103 calories, contains only 2.3 grams of protein. Therefore, the meat, although weak in calories, contains three times the tissue building material found in hominy.

Trial, experience and results, rather than

136 HEREDITY AND CHILD CULTURE

mere theory, must prove the final test of the utility of any plan of nutrition.

Under-Nourished Children

Attention has recently been directed to the large number of growing children who are suffering from various grades of mal-nutrition. This condition is not confined to any one class since it is seen as often among the well-to-do as among the poor. We are largely indebted to Dr. William R. P. Emerson of Boston for an investigation of this subject. These children are often anæmic, languid, easily fatigued, highly nervous or irritable, and do not seem to fit in well with their environment. The condition is often caused by faulty habits of eating as well as by badly regulated diets. The immediate effect is not only disastrous, but mal-nutrition at this time is the cause of many ills in later life. According to tests made in various localities, Dr. Emerson believes that from 20 to 40 per cent. of children at the pre-school and school age in America show physical and mental signs of mal-nutrition. One of the surest methods of recognising this condition consists in observing the relation between weight and height, as children who are habitually underweight for their height may

PROPER NUTRITION 137

usually be considered as under-nourished. In considering what range of variation may be compatible with health, 10 per cent. of under weight is taken as a working hypothesis by Dr. Emerson, as shown in the following table,—

Height Inches	Average Weight for Height Pounds	10% Under Weight Pounds	Average Weight for Height Pounds	10% Under Weight Pounds
		BOYS		GIRLS
21	8.2	7.4	7.9	7.1
22	9.7	8.7	9.4	8.5
23	11.1	10.0	11.0	9.9
24	12.5	11.3	12.5	11.3
25	13.9	12.5	14.0	12.6
26	15.3	13.8	15.5	14.0
27	16.9	15.2	17.2	15.5
28	18.5	16.7	18.8	16.9
29	20.2	18.2	20.5	18.5
30	21.7	19.6	22.0	19.8
31	23.2	20.9	23.4	21.1
32	24.5	22.1	24.8	22.3
33	25.9	23.3	26.0	23.4
34	27.3	24.6	27.3	24.6
35	28.7	25.8	28.6	25.7
36	30.0	27.0	30.0	27.0
37	31.6	28.4	31.5	28.4
38	33.2	29.9	32.7	29.4
39	36.3	32.7	35.7	32.1
40	38.1	34.3	37.4	33.7
41	39.8	35.8	39.2	35.3
42	41.7	37.5	41.2	37.1
43	43.5	39.2	43.1	38.8
44	45.4	40.9	44.8	40.3
45	47.1	42.4	46.3	41.7
46	49.5	44.6	48.5	43.7
47	51.4	46.3	50.9	45.8
48	53.0	47.7	53.3	48.0
49	55.4	49.9	55.8	50.2
50	59.6	53.6	58.3	52.5
51	62.5	56.3	61.1	55.0
52	65.8	59.2	63.8	57.4
53	68.9	62.0	66.8	60.1
54	72.0	64.8	70.3	63.3
55	75.4	67.9	74.5	67.1
56	79.2	71.3	78.4	70.6

138 HEREDITY AND CHILD CULTURE

Height Inches	Average Weight for Height Pounds	10% Under Weight Pounds	Average Weight for Height Pounds	10% Under Weight Pounds
		BOYS		GIRLS
57	82.8	74.5	82.5	74.3
58	87.0	78.3	86.6	77.9
59	91.1	82.0	91.1	82.0
60	95.2	85.7	96.7	87.0
61	99.3	89.4	102.5	99.2
62	103.8	93.4	110.4	99.4
63	108.0	97.2	118.0	106.2
64	114.7	103.2	123.0	110.7
65	121.8	109.6	130.0	117.0
66	127.8	115.0	137.0	123.3
67	132.6	119.3	143.0	128.7
68	138.9	125.0	146.9	132.2

A child whose weight does not agree with its height and who is 10 per cent. under weight is not well nourished. These figures, however, are only averages, and do not apply to exceptional cases. Still they will prove valuable in leading to a careful study of all the life conditions of a child showing such irregularity. It is especially when growth is very active that under feeding or wrong feeding is most disastrous. Adolescence is the time that especially requires a most liberal diet. Quick growth and marked muscular and glandular activity call for abundant food. Sometimes children who are properly fed but who are over-active in study or play become under nourished. Dr. Emerson stresses the importance of rest periods for under weight children in addition to regulation of diet. This was well exemplified in a

PROPER NUTRITION 139

class of under nourished children under my observation in one of the public schools of New York. An abundant dinner was furnished these children, of which all partook. A number, however, failed to gain. When a rest period of an hour after dinner was added to the régime, these same children gained also. General hygienic oversight is therefore required in dealing with such children. The first necessity is to stop habits that interfere with healthy appetite and digestion. The eating of candy and sweets, the drinking of tea and coffee, and other dietetic errors must first be corrected before improvement can be expected.

CHAPTER XIII

THE FAMILY

IT is a truism to remark that the welfare of the child is closely bound up with that of the family. Any influence that weakens the status of the family and the home is at once disastrously reflected upon the developing child. The necessity for strengthening and conserving family relations, as far as possible, in all individual and social endeavours is not only shown in beneficial practical results but has a deep philosophic reason as well. The family stands at the foundation of the complete fabric of civilization.

John Fiske elaborates this thought in his *Outlines of Cosmic Philosophy*, and it may be of interest to quote some of his words,—"The feature by which the most rudimentary human family group is distinguished from any collocation of kindred individuals among gregarious mammals is the permanent character of the relationships between its constituent members. Enduring from birth until death, these

THE FAMILY 141

relationships acquire a traditionary value which passes on from generation to generation, and thus there arise reciprocal necessities of behaviour between parents and children, husbands and wives, brothers and sisters, in which reciprocal necessities of behaviour, we have discerned the requisite conditions for the genesis of those egoaltruistic impulses which, when further modified by the expansion of sympathetic feelings, give birth to moral sentiments. * * * * * We bridge the gulf which seems, on a superficial view, forever to divide the human from the brute world. And not least, in the grand result, is the profound meaning which is given to the phenomena of helpless babyhood. From of old we have heard the monition, 'Except ye be as babes, ye cannot enter the kingdom of heaven.' The latest science now shows us—though in a very different sense of the word—that, unless we had been as babes, the ethical phenomena which gives all its significance to the phrase 'kingdom of heaven' would have been non-existent for us. Without the circumstances of infancy we might have become formidable among animals through sheer force of sharp-wittedness. But, except for these circumstances, we should never have comprehended the meaning of such phrases as 'self-sacrifices,' or 'devotion.'

142 HEREDITY AND CHILD CULTURE

The phenomena of social life would have been omitted from the history of the world, and with them the phenomena of ethics and religion."

While the bringing up and training of the child call for watchful care and constant labour, if it be conscientiously and hopefully undertaken, there are the greatest rewards and compensations for such efforts. It is only necessary to note what the child does for parents and the race to see how this must be so. In the scheme of higher evolution the child stands pre-eminent. It was the maternal care required by the long period of helpless infancy that first initiated altruism into the human race. It takes time to develop unselfishness and sympathy, and in the lower animals the interval requiring such complete care and self-sacrifice is lacking. It is the helpless child that develops in the mother carefulness, patience and tenderness; if these do not exist in her, the child cannot survive. Merely bringing a child into life is not sufficient, so that an ethical element is as necessary as a physical one for continued existence.

The human child does what the offspring of the lower animals never accomplishes—it acts as a developer of the affections—it creates the true mother. Every mother may thus become

THE FAMILY 143

a Madonna.   The greatest moral force in the world for its uplifting hence has its original basis in a physical condition in which the child plays the leading rôle.   Drummond[1] calls attention to the fact that before maternal love can be evolved out of mere rudimentary care, before love can be made a necessity and carried past the unhatched egg to the living thing which is to come out of it, nature must alter all her ways.   He puts it thus—" Four great changes at least must be introduced into her programme. In the first place, she must cause fewer young to be produced at birth.   In the second place, she must have these young produced in such outward form that their mothers will recognise them.   In the third place, instead of producing them in such physical perfection that they are able to go out into life the moment they are born, she must make them helpless, so that for a time they must dwell with her if they are to live at all.   And, fourthly, it is required that she shall be made to dwell with them ; that in some way they also should be made necessary, —physically necessary—to her to compel her to attend to them.   All these beautiful arrangements we find carried out to the last detail."   The human mother is thus primarily made by these

[1] *The Ascent of Man,* James Pott & Co,

144 HEREDITY AND CHILD CULTURE

four processes. During this period the mother also requires care and protection, and thus is evolved the father, giving love and support to mother and offspring. In this way the family is created, which is the unit of civilization around which cluster all the higher attributes of man.

Love, apart from passion and selfishness, is due to children ; it has descended directly from them. The nurture and care of children, if properly conceived and carried out, constitute the great educators in the character of parents. For children give more than they take. They are the greatest civilizers and humanizers of the race. Without their unconscious but beneficial influence, we would soon relapse into a possibly refined but selfish barbarism. The child has done more for the regeneration of the race than all the creeds that have ever been formulated.

As the best physical, moral and social development of child-life takes place in the individual home, every effort must be made to strengthen and conserve family life. The child forms the connective link of the family, which, in turn, represents the earliest human unit of association, antedating both church and state. In fact, the earliest form of government found

THE FAMILY 145

expression in the patriarchal family. In social evolution, the monogamous relationship exhibits the highest form that family life has attained. It is probable that promiscuity marked the life of primitive man. Among many early tribes and nations, the family in the modern sense cannot be said to have functioned. The ideal of monogamous marriage puts the home as the centre of family life, and all must recognize that here is the best place for child training. The home properly organized also elevates women and promotes religion. All remedial efforts, both individual and social, must begin in the home, and, if results are to be enduring, must likewise end there.

As the child has done so much in the evolution of the family and of civilization itself, it is evident that parents have a most important duty in training the young and developing a normal family life. To this end, parents should see more of their children in order to study their individual needs and possibilities. Too often they are early relegated to nurses and governesses, and later to pedagogues who cannot have the personal interest that should be possessed by parents.

During infancy and early childhood, the mother is frequently willing to trust the child

K

146 HEREDITY AND CHILD CULTURE

to an ignorant nursemaid of the peasant type, who has not had a proper training for this important service. Preparation and education are required for all callings and professions except the most important one of all,—that of caring for little children. The mothers themselves are the natural ones to give the major care to their young children, or, if desiring help, should have the knowledge and character to properly direct the nurse. Babies grow fond of those who personally minister to their wants, and it is pathetic to see an infant turn away from a refined mother and cry for some coarse, ignorant but kindly woman who feeds and cares for it. A little later, vulgar language and undesirable habits may be acquired by such close association.

There is no nobler profession in the world than that of mother. Like all callings in the modern world, it demands efficiency. While women have striven for advancement in all phases of present day activities,—science, art, literature and social organization, they have often not kept pace with a wiser regimen in the rearing of children. It might be well to establish schools of motherhood where, based upon a general foundation of biology, the students could be taught the hygiene, physio-

THE FAMILY 147

logy and psychology of childhood. If such knowledge could be applied, it would not take many generations to secure a better, sounder race. Such a school might confer a degree that would be equivalent to that obtained by becoming proficient in ancient history or the parallelopiped of forces. Much of the underlying restlessness and discontent in life, so often seen among our better-favoured women would soon disappear if they could obtain a fresh orientation by studying and helping the little child. The average father has also an important duty, too often neglected, in studying and directing his children. He is so immersed in the business of making money to care for their material wants, that he has little or no time to guide their mental and spiritual development in the right direction. The social engagements of the mother, and the business preoccupations of the father, result in no time being left for the children. They are thus sent to boarding-schools and summer camps, and the whole duty of oversight shifted to the pedagogue. It is time more parents themselves attended to the difficult and serious work of raising their offspring.

One of the greatest evils of divorce, that is now unfortunately so prevalent, is the total

148 HEREDITY AND CHILD CULTURE

disregard of the real interest of children. The breaking-up of the home and handing them out from one parent to the other in six-month shifts has a most disastrous effect. The inherent selfishness of the men aud women who stand for this practice is appalling.

What is much needed among all classes at the present time is more of an appreciation of the great responsibility of bringing children into the world, and the necessity of giving them a wholesome, happy family life. It is only thus that a normal, healthy generation can be reared.

Some of our advanced communistic philosophers have lately proposed that children be separated from their parents and brought up in huge caravansaries under the care of the state. These pseudo-thinkers are as ignorant of biology as of experience. Their pronouncements are better fitted for the barnyard than for civilized society. All experience shows that the highest development of the child takes place in the individual family and home.

The trend away from the home is one of the evils of the day, and must be checked if future civilization is not to become retrogressive. The family must be conserved at any cost if only for the benefit of the child.

CHAPTER XIV

THE DEPENDENT CHILD

THE abandoned, dependent child forms a problem that has been poorly solved by modern society. We have warnings that some of our methods of child care are not the best. Those who thoughtfully work for dependent infants and children have long felt stirrings of discontent with the methods in common use. We need a fresh orientation to guide our efforts in newer and more productive channels. A new spirit is called for which is not easy to find, and in which the *individual needs* of every neglected child will be considered. In this period of general reconstruction, let us try and put the salvage of abandoned, dependent children on a natural and secure basis. To this end all remedial efforts should be planned, as far as possible, along the line of Nature's laws.

It is only necessary to glance at some of the methods employed to understand why results have been so unsatisfactory. Many years ago needy children were sent to poor-houses, with or without their parents as the case might be.

150 HEREDITY AND CHILD CULTURE

This plan worked badly ; subsequently, they were boarded out in a careless, haphazard manner. The old baby-farming experience at once comes to mind, where an ignorant woman, living in squalor, took as many babies to board as she could accommodate, with a sick and death-rate that was appalling. The late Dr. Elisha Harris, once reporting on this subject, stated that in New York, from 1854 to 1859, about 1000 infants were boarded out each year, and ninety out of one hundred did not live to see their first birthday. As this plan was so deplorable it was determined to house this class of children in large institutions where doctors and nurses could hold sway and try for better results. But when some years later this same class of infants was collected in an institution on Randall's Island, the results with young infants were frequently worse, as the death-rate often reached 95 per cent. if they were kept very long.

In this gradual evolution of saving destitute children, the pathway, with many digressions, started at the almshouse ; next followed the plan of careless farming out, and then came the congregate and cottage institution. Finally we have some sort of boarding out as the best solution of a very difficult problem.

THE DEPENDENT CHILD 151

The public systems for the care of dependent children by the various states have been classified by Homer Folks as follows : [1]

1. The state school and placing-out system, adopted by Michigan, Minnesota, Wisconsin, Rhode Island, Kansas, Colorado, Nebraska, Montana, Nevada and Texas. While the children may first be collected in an institution, the aim of this system is to place them in actual homes as soon as possible.

2. The county children's home system. adopted by Ohio, Connecticut and Indiana. While placing-out is practised to some extent, it is not an important feature of this system,

3. The plan of supporting public charges in private institutions, which prevails in New York, California, Maryland, District of Columbia, and to some extent in several other states. By per capita payments this plan encourages a long retention and building up of large institutions with a discouragement of placing-out.

4. The boarding-out and placing-out system, which is carried on directly by the public authorities in Massachusetts ; through a private organization—the Children's Aid

---

[1] *The Care of Neglected, Destitute and Delinquent Children,* The Macmillan Co.

152 HEREDITY AND CHILD CULTURE

Society—in Pennsylvania; and has recently been undertaken by the state authorities in New Jersey.

Thus in three states dependent children are directly boarded-out in family homes, followed by efforts made to place them in permanent free homes. This plan was earliest developed in Massachusetts, where it has been successfully carried out on a large scale since 1882, when the children began to be removed from the state primary school. The latter was entirely abolished in 1895, since which time all the state dependent children have been boarded out. Three years later (1898) the city of Boston likewise abandoned the institutional plan and placed all destitute children in family homes.

It is the infant that suffers most from institutional care. Babies are brought into the world singly and not in droves, and they crave individual care and mothering. The little child craves love. That close human observer, Jane Addams, with sympathetic vision, puts it thus:—
" We are told that the will to live is aroused in each baby by his mother's irresistable desire to play with him, the physiological value of joy that a child is born, and that the high death-rate in institutions is increased by the discontented babies whom no one persuades into living."

THE DEPENDENT CHILD 153

In the last report of the State Board of Charities of New York it is stated that 57.2 per cent. of infants under one year died in infant asylums throughout the state. There have been similar results as long as records have been kept. Under three months, the mortality often reaches two-thirds of the cases admitted. Some years ago the American Child Hygiene Association reported that during a series of years the general death rate of children under two years in the State of New York was about one-fifth that of institutions. It is only fair to add that they frequently receive abandoned infants in a weakened condition, and that such cases are hard to manage. The bad results are not due to lack of kindness or attention, but to the fact that the whole system is wrong.[1] Good motives and bad methods may co-exist. It often requires the work of the wise to correct the mistakes of the good.

[1] To those who are specially interested, reference is made to the following articles I have written on this subject :

"A Plan of Dealing with Atrophic Infants and Children." *Archives of Pediatrics*, July, 1908.

"The Proper Management of Foundlings and Neglected Infants." *N.Y. Med. Record*, February 18, 1911.

"Are Institutes for Infants Necessary?" *Jour. A.M.A.*, January 2, 1915.

"A Plea for Accurate Statistics in Infant's Institutions." *Archives of Pediatrics*, October, 1915.

"A Scheme of State Control for Dependent Infants." *N.Y. Med. Record*, June 17, 1916.

154 HEREDITY AND CHILD CULTURE

Aside from the large death-rate, there is much sickness in the institutions, due largely to contact infections. It seems impossible to avoid manifold cross infections when those susceptible infants are handled in mass. They have a low resistance ; all kinds of colds, especially of the influenza type, spread unchecked, and many cases of bronchitis and bronco-pneumonia are thus contracted. If the specific contagions, such as measles, scarlet-fever, whooping-cough or chicken-pox gain access to an institution, as they very frequently do, they spread like wild fire, and the results are often most disastrous.

There is also constant danger in children's hospitals, as well as asylums, from the entrance and spread of these infections. I do not approve of the multiplication of infants' and children's hospitals through the country. A few can do all the necessary work. In most cases, a small ward in a general hospital can function efficiently and economically for sick

---

"Systematized Boarding Out *v*. Institutional Care for Infants and Young Children." *N. Y. Med. Journal*, June 2, 1917.

"The Speedwell Plan of Child Saving in Theory and Practice." *The Survey*, October 26, 1918.

"Problems of Boarding-out, with an Attempted Solution." *N. Y. Med. Record*, April 24, 1920.

A little volume entitled, *The Traffic in Babies*, by George Walker, M.D., published by the Norman Remington Company, Baltimore, makes startling reading.

THE DEPENDENT CHILD 155

children requiring special care. The hospital need only be utilized for surgical operations, for severe illnesses requiring highly specialized nursing and treatment, and for scientific observation of obscure cases requiring much laboratory study. Children, and especially infants, do not respond well to prolonged hospital care. As soon as acute symptoms of disease have passed, they should be promptly discharged. Otherwise, there is liable to be recurrence of the original disease or a succumbing to some communicable infection. Convalescence should take place elsewhere.

Recognizing this fact, in 1890 I started Hospital Social Service in connection with the children's division of the New York Post-Graduate Hospital. After a quick discharge, the necessary medical, surgical and social after-care takes place in the home. I believe this represents the first activity of the kind to be started and kept up as a routine proceeding.[1] In this connection it is interesting to note that the nurses of the Henry Street Settlement of New York got better results with certain diseases of childhood, notably pneumonia, treated at home than do any of the hospitals.

[1] "The Relation Between the Child and Hospital Social Service"— *Journal of the American Medical Association*, July 23, 1921.

156 HEREDITY AND CHILD CULTURE

Aside from infection the infants in institutions often progressively lose weight and lie in rows of cots in an apathetic condition, as there are usually too few attendants to take them up for needed change and exercise. It is especially at night that babies may lie unattended from this cause. They rarely get enough fresh outside air : oxygen is needed as well as food to keep them in vigour. All these factors result in the devitalized babies so often seen in institutions. In warm climates they suffer much less from confinement in institutions, owing to the fact that windows may be kept open and their cots can be placed on porches or in courtyards.

Owing to the facts here noted, the drift of opinion among thoughful workers is strongly against the collective management of these cases, especially when the numbers are large. There has been an extraordinary agreement on this question among those who have had the widest opportunity for observation and experiment.

As far back as 1909, a conference on the care of dependent children was held at Washington D.C., at the call of President Roosevelt, who was much interested in this vital human problem. A large number of practical workers and experts in child saving from all parts of the

THE DEPENDENT CHILD 157

country took part in the deliberations of this conference. Among many conclusions reached upon diverse problems of child saving, the following especially concern us here : " Home life is the highest and finest product of civilization. It is the great moulding force of mind and character. Children should not be deprived of it except for urgent and compelling reasons. * * * * * * As to the children who for sufficient reasons must be removed from their own homes, or who have no homes, it is desirable that, if normal in mind or body, and not requiring special training, they should be cared for in families whenever practicable. The carefully selected foster home is for the normal child the best substitute for the natural home." We have thus represented in these words the national opinion on this subject.

Ten years later an International Conference of Red Cross Societies, held at Cannes, gave what can fairly be said to represent the best world thought on this question : " Permanent institutional care for infants and young children should be discouraged on account of the almost insuperable difficulties in maintaining nutrition in infancy under these conditions and because of the great susceptibility of young children to

158 HEREDITY AND CHILD CULTURE

infection ; preference should be given to placing such children in suitable families."

Two experiments might be mentioned in which a striking difference between institutional and home care of abandoned infants has been recorded. In San Francisco the mortality for years in the foundling asylums averaged 50 per cent. The authorities of these institutions finally consented to abandon the institutional care and resorted to boarding out with careful oversight. A group of young college women undertook the follow-up work, and once a week all the babies are brought to a central station for weighing and general advice. As a result, the mortality of this class of cases has been reduced to 12 per cent.

A more striking comparison between institutional and boarding out mortality is afforded by the results obtained by the Sage Foundation and the Department of Health with babies taken from the marasmus ward of the N.Y. Foundling hospital.[1] This ward receives only the chronic cases of extreme atrophy that have always ended in death. In boarding out a number of these babies, an extra bonus was given to selected women, and a doctor and a nurse furnished for every ten babies. As a

[1] *Woman's Medical Journal*, Jan. 1916.

THE DEPENDENT CHILD

result there was an eventual mortality of 46 per cent. Thus nearly half of the babies were saved in the home who were bound to die in the institution.

As expert opinion is in such wide agreement upon stressing of family homes rather than the institution in the care of the abandoned young, it is strange that more thought and effort have not been placed on the problems of boarding out. The latter has not always functioned as well as it should, owing to lack of proper oversight and regulation.

The two main difficulties of boarding out consist, first in selecting a suitable home, and next in exercising constant and proper supervision. Where boarding out has fallen short, one or both of these factors have not been sufficiently emphazied.

The Speedwell System

After much thought on this subject in 1902, I developed what is known as the Speedwell System, that represents a sustained effort so to regulate and systematize boarding out as to place its good effects at a maximum and its possible bad effects at a minimum. This has been accomplished by developing what may be called a unit system of intensive boarding out.

160 HEREDITY AND CHILD CULTURE

A unit consists of a neighbourhood selected after a survey has been made to learn the general conditions of healthfulness and the number of good homes available in the locality. There is then inaugurated a constant oversight, especially as to diet and hygiene, on the part of a salaried physician and nurse who are thoroughly familiar with this class of cases and competent to deal with them. The children are kept indefinitely until digestion and assimilation have improved sufficiently to result in a permanent increase in weight and strength.

Efforts are made to train in each neighbourhood a number of foster-mothers, who, by natural aptitude under instruction and by constantly taking infants and young children into their homes, become fairly expert in handling them under conditions totally unlike those offered by institutions and far superior to them. We thus try to carry on an important educational work among the families taking our children. The constant oversight of our doctor and nurse is aimed to help each foster mother in the care of her own children as well. The homes in which the children are placed are helped financially by the board paid, and morally by the good advice and watching of the trained observers.

THE DEPENDENT CHILD 161

Thus the simple machinery that endeavours to really and permanently help the abandoned and ailing child will, at the same time, assist in educating each community in which it operates in prevention and care of its own ailing children. This by-product, involving improved social ideals and a higher standard of living, may be made a very important feature of this work. It need hardly be stated that this individual and social ideal, in order to attain its highest success, must be operated by those who believe in it and are willing to put forth enthusiastic efforts toward its support. In other words, the human effort is here the important factor, and the system, in order to attain its greatest efficiency, calls for high grade workers who can idealize their efforts, as well as for good family homes where the boarded-out children will be reared under constant and intelligent supervision. The emphasis is thus placed on *human agents* rather than on bricks and mortar.

The underlying idea of a unit is to include a certain area in city or country that will be sufficiently circumscribed to allow the workers to be acquainted with the personnel of the neighbourhood and accessible for communication. It may include a part or the whole

162 HEREDITY AND CHILD CULTURE

of a village or a certain district or a ward in a city.

The formation of a unit involves first the selection of a number of promising homes after the preliminary survey. Our experience has shown that it is a mistake to be too fastidious at first in selecting the homes. If the woman of the household has motherly instincts and fairly healthy children of her own, and seems teachable, a certain amount of dirt and disorder can well be overlooked at the start. A porch or back yard, or some open space, is most essential, as plenty of fresh air is one of the important features of this work.

The next step is to select a committee of women living in or near the locality selected for the unit, who are familiar with the neighbourhood and the people, and who constitute the local managers of the undertaking. They may help in raising money and supplies, assist in friendly visiting in the homes, acquaint themselves with neighbourhood conditions and in these and other ways exercise general supervision of the work. A further possibility of this endeavour may be to enable the well-to-do classes to properly envisage the life conditions of those less favoured and thereby to develop genuine human relationships.

THE DEPENDENT CHILD 163

The records kept of the children are uniform in all the units, and careful histories on a card system show the conditions and results of their care.

There is a unit at Morristown, N.J., one at Yonkers, N.Y., and one at New Rochelle, N.Y., operated by the Free Synagogue of New York, which prepares abandoned children for adoption in Jewish homes. There is now being started a unit in the Kingsbridge section of New York City. The results as shown by a lowered death-rate, and the production of healthy normal children proves the superiority of this system over other plans of child saving. Each large city can be surrounded by units, and also have units, as well as collecting stations, in town. A rough outline of existing units is shown by the first two diagrams, while the third illustrates our ideal for the general extension of the work.

On the economic side, it is cheaper, as there are no overhead expenses for the operation of buildings requiring service and supplies. In figuring institution expense, the cost of the plant and equipment, as well as the remitted taxes must be included.

The Speedwell system can be indefinitely enlarged by the simple multiplication of units,

164 HEREDITY AND CHILD CULTURE

all operating on the same plan, and only requiring as the work enlarges a central registry for temporary reception and distribution of cases. One or two rooms in a tenement house could serve the purpose.

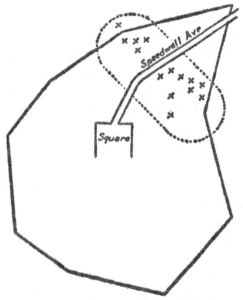

Fig. 1. Outline of Morristown Unit.

In this system which has been in successful operation for twenty years, I believe we have the best solution of a baffling problem. It has responded to the pragmatic test,—it works.

At the International Congress for Child Welfare recently held in Brussels, the Congress recommended the organization throughout Europe of the unit method of boarding out, as operated by the Speedwell System in the United States.

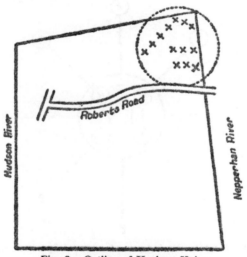

Fig. 2. Outline of Yonkers Unit.

While older children do not suffer as do infants in mortality and morbidity from institutional life they are under abnormal conditions if they stay too long in such a place. The defective or delinquent child is best handled in an institution, but all others do better outside. The mass training of defectives is often more effective than individual care.

166 HEREDITY AND CHILD CULTURE

Professor E. P. Devine[1] states that while in some places institutions seem necessary, yet they should not be encouraged, as they are wasteful of child life, wasteful of economic

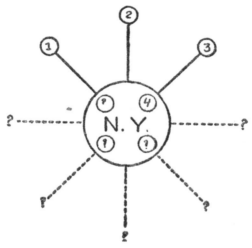

Fig. 3. Diagram showing present extent of Speedwell work and possibilities of expansion.
(1) Morristown Unit.
(2) Yonkers Unit.
(3) New Rochelle Unit.
(4) City Unit (Kingsbridge).
(?) Other possible units in town and country.

efficiency and character, promotive often of a spirit the opposite of law abiding, and this because they do not give an experience to the

[1] "*The Normal Life*"—Survey Associates.

THE DEPENDENT CHILD   167

child in natural family and neighbourhood relationships, do not give an opportunity for the development of self-reliance and self-direction, do not gradually initiate the child into the every day routine of free citizenship, but necessarily repress his budding individuality, limit and control the exercise of his judgment as to his body, contract his vision, mutilate his faculties and distort his sense of values.

Professor Devine reaches the following conclusion,—"It is the large institution under private or religious auspices, managed by a self-perpetuating or appointed board, but supported by state or municipal appropriations, which is most difficult to keep human and educational. To keep within reasonable bounds as to size, or within reasonable bounds as to its subtle influence on state and municipal affairs. The subsidy or contract system continually grows by what it feeds on. It represents an unsound principle of divorcing control from support. One body directs the affairs of the institution ; another pays the bills. The result is a division of responsibility and the neglect of the child."

There are times when it is difficult to avoid placing children in institutions, but in such

168 HEREDITY AND CHILD CULTURE

cases the stay should be as short as possible, and, as the cottage plan does away with some of the evils, it should be the one of choice. The old congregate system, where children are housed in large dormitories, should be abandoned. The inmates too often lose all individual initiative and become little automatons. The spread of evil habits and associations can occur very easily under institutional auspices. Thomas Mott Osborne has said that many of his wards at Sing Sing Prison had their early training in institutions. He recently told me that a study of a group of prisoners at Auburn once showed that two-thirds of them had previously been inmates of juvenile institutions.

It is thus evident that every effort should be made to keep children out of large institutions. So far as the child is concerned, the United States is institution-ridden, as there are relatively more here than in any other country. Scotland has the honour of maintaining the fewest. If parents die or are utterly unable to care for their children, some form of boarding out should be employed. The Speedwell plan can work with older as well as younger children, as it does away with the usual objection to boarding out—lack of constant oversight.

THE DEPENDENT CHILD 169

A very great advance has been made in solving the problem of widows with children. Miss Loeb[1] has stated that the local governments in 41 states have now solved this question by entering widows' homes and seeing to it that the dependent children have that home influence which is most essential in the rearing of citizens. A Widows' Pension Law has been enacted in these states after the deliberations of a commission charged with the work of investigating the subject. Thus, instead of removing dependent children from their own mothers and paying institutions to care for them, the money is paid to the mother herself and the home thereby kept intact. It is further stated by Miss Loeb that during the first six months of a recent year, New York City cared for 16,526 children together with their mothers : for the same period, 20,868 children were housed in private institutions. Aside from the great humanitarian element involved, it cost New York nearly twice as much to keep children in institutional homes as compared with the cost of keeping them in the private homes of their mothers.

The magnitude and importance of the problem raised by the abandoned child has not

[1] *Everyman's Child*—The Century Co.

170 HEREDITY AND CHILD CULTURE

been sufficiently realized. Last year, in New York State alone, 31,177 dependent children were being trained and housed in institutions. Are these little lives being badly warped from unnatural surroundings? Shall they later become assets or liabilities to the community? We must always remember that children constitute the greatest possible future asset of the State. If they are improperly nurtured, society will later be obliged to build other institutions for protection. It is cheaper and wiser to try to raise the child in a wholesome, normal manner. To this end, everything must be done to conserve the home. Children must be educated and the parents re-educated, if necessary, along normal lines. The great responsibility of parenthood and the importance of conserving family relationships must be inculcated. In some instances, shiftless parents are encouraged too easily to cast off responsibility for their children.

For the abandoned, dependent child, sympathetic care according to its needs must be rendered. An increasing knowledge of the real requirements of child life will not tolerate faulty methods much longer, for a larger and wiser human spirit is at work on these problems, which is not content to put up with evils that

THE DEPENDENT CHILD   **171**

can be prevented. A wider vision, truer courage, and broader human feeling is needed in this work. The results will be worthy of the effort.

The most powerful forces of nature, such as heat, electricity or the all-embracing ether, are subtle and unseen ; may we not include mother love as another most potent agency in creating and sustaining life ?

Phillips Brooks says very wisely,—" He who helps a child helps humanity with a distinctness, with an immediateness, which no other help given to human creatures in any other stage of their human life can possibly give again."

CHAPTER XV

THE ADOPTION OF CHILDREN

ATTENTION has been directed in a previous chapter to the fact that the poorest families usually have the largest number of children. If sickness or death comes to such a family, to cripple or remove the bread winner, the children are often stranded and the community must then come to the rescue. In many instances, the institution steps in and affords the needed refuge.

On the other hand, many people in easy or independent circumstances, have few or no children. This is not entirely due to birth control, as is usually supposed. In many cases, it is owing to physical causes that are troublesome or impossible of removal. Civilization is hard on women and the higher they are in the social scale, the more difficult and uncertain becomes the question of maternity. If some of the surplus children at one end of the social scale could be transferred to the opposite end, the result would be most beneficial. This

THE ADOPTION OF CHILDREN 173

means that the homeless child should be placed in a childless home, to the lasting benefit of both.

There is always going on a social current moving from below upward; too high a degree of civilization often has a devitalizing influence on both the individual and society. There is some truth in the old adage that it takes three generations to get from shirtsleeves to shirtsleeves.

It is not only in married homes which are childless that the adoption of children would be beneficial. If well-to-do spinsters would take one or two children and bring them up in their homes, there would be less neurasthenia and hysteria in this class. The maternal instinct is often highly developed in unmarried women, and this plan would afford it a normal and useful outlet.

A vigorous stream of life may thus be made to flow into some of our older families by engrafting children who, although having a poor social inheritance, may yet be the possessors of a healthy organic inheritance. As a matter of fact, our oldest and so-called best families often cannot be safe in looking too closely into their ancestry. Many of the proudest families in Europe are descended from glorified cut-

174 HEREDITY AND CHILD CULTURE

throats whose only claim to distinction lay in slaughtering the peasants of neighbouring countries. The best known families of our own democracy have had forebears who engaged in the useful though humble occupations of stage-drivers, ferrymen, and fur traders.

It is also a fact that individuals of the same race are more nearly related than is generally supposed. The following is a quotation from Conklin : "Davenport concludes that no people of English descent are more distantly related than thirtieth cousins, while most people are much more closely related than that." If there is a good organic heredity behind any child, a favourable environment will do the rest.

It is thus wise and safe to encourage the adoption of abandoned children who are normal and healthy. The beneficial effect will follow not only to the child but to the family taking it in.

The adoption of children goes back to great antiquity. The Babylonians had laws for its regulation, as mentioned in the Code of Hammarubi composed 2285 B.C. Mr. John Francis Brosnan,[1] of the New York bar, has written an interesting monograph upon this subject from which the following excerpts are taken—"Look-

[1] *The Medical Times*, June, 1917.

THE ADOPTION OF CHILDREN 175

ing first to Rome, the admitted source of our law on this subject, we find that from its earliest days the civil law recognised adoption. At first it was attended with great ceremonial dignity. Later, Justinian simplified and codified its procedure. Originally accomplished by authority of the people assembled in Comita, it later became effective by imperial rescript or by a proceeding before a magistrate wherein appeared personally the person giving, the person given, and the person receiving. The results were far reaching. Not only the person adopted came under the power of the person adopting him, but the power given to the adopting father extended over the children and the grandchildren of the person adopted. * * * * From Roman law quite naturally the practice became incorporated in the jurisprudence of the Latin races. In ancient epochs it was prevalent in some portions of France, but not permitted in others. It seems to have been of varying kinds. There was a form whereby a man took the name of the person adopting him and agreed to bear arms in his behalf. This did not give him any new property rights. * * * * The Code Napoleon, which crystallized the French law, did not provide for an absolute change of family. Indeed, it did not permit the adoption of minors,

176 HEREDITY AND CHILD CULTURE

but prepared the way for adoption by creating what was termed an official tutorship. By the Spanish law the person adopted succeeded as heir to the one adopting him. * * * * The Assyrians, the Greeks, and the Egyptians all recorded it. In Greece, in the interests of the next of kin, it was provided that the ceremony should be attended with certain formalities and take place at the time of certain festivals. Among the Egyptians we have the historic a-doption of Moses, set forth in the words of Holy Writ—'And she adopted him for a son and called him Moses, saying I took him out of the water.' The Hebrew law is silent on the subject. Some writers have urged that the words of St. Paul show that it was well known to them, but it is submitted that these similes were painted by the great apostle for the Romans and the Galatians, people who knew and practised adoption. Adoption among the ancient Germans was attended with military ceremonies and the placing of warlike weapons in the hands of the adopted. * * * * We find it among the tribal customs of the Indians of the Western World. * * * * While adoption is now general in the United States, it was not until the middle half of the nineteenth century that statutes changing the common law so as to

THE ADOPTION OF CHILDREN 177

permit the same were enacted, Massachusetts, in 1851, being the first of the common law States to pass the same."

Statutes permitting and regulating adoption are now in force in most of the states of the Union. The legal relations are the same as those that exist between natural parents and children, including control, obedience and inheritance rights. In some states an order of the court is required, while in others a deed acknowledged and recorded is sufficient to consummate the adoption.

The following excerpts are taken from the New York State law: "The foster parent or parents, the person to be adopted, and all the persons whose consent is necessary * * * must appear before the County judge or the surrogate of the county where the foster parent or parents reside and be examined by such judge or surrogate. * * * * If satisfied that the moral and temporal interests of the person to be adopted will be promoted thereby, the judge or surrogate must make an order allowing and confirming such adoption, reciting the reasons therefor, and directing that the person to be adopted shall thenceforth be regarded and treated in all respects as the child of the foster parent or parents."

M

178 HEREDITY AND CHILD CULTURE

England is one of the few civilized countries that has no adoption laws and never has had any. It is strange that since the War, with all the orphans and war babies needing homes, this great legal defect has not been corrected by act of parliament.

There are various ways in which children are received and offered for adoption. The orphan and juvenile asylums have usually a larger or smaller number of children who are available for adoption. It is often difficult to get them out, however, owing to religious and other qualifications that are not easy to fulfil. Some of the large Societies having close relationships with children, such as the State Charities Aid Association and Children's Aid Society of New York, also have as an important feature of their work the adoption of children. Since 1898 the former Society has placed 3400 children in homes for adoption ; in the last six years, the latter organization has done the same beneficent work for 432 children, and the great majority have turned out well. It is a most satisfactory and promising kind of remedial effort, as the results are constructive and permanent. The greater the number of agencies that will attack this problem, the more widespread and flexible will be the efforts and results,

THE ADOPTION OF CHILDREN 179

In 1910 my wife, wishing especially to help this class of cases, began taking abandoned infants and little children into our home to prepare them for adoption. To our surprise, there was a greater demand for these little waifs than we could readily supply. Accordingly, the Alice Chapin Adoption Nursery was launched in an apartment where eight babies at a time are nurtured with adoption in view. Over four hundred children have been placed in good homes all over the country since the beginning of this work. Some of the features came as an additional surprise. It is understood that any child can be returned within a year, and yet among this large number only eight have been sent back. In these returned cases the fault lay more with the foster parents than with the children, as other and more satisfactory placements were soon made for the latter. It is astonishing how soon close and tender relationships are established between the foster parents and these children. It early becomes as unthinkable to separate them as if they were their own children. They are proudly exhibited and their good points paraded in quite the orthodox paternal and maternal manner. They have brought life and brightness into drab homes; neurotic women have forgotten their peculiar

180 HEREDITY AND CHILD CULTURE

ailments in watching the child develop. It forms a very satisfactory "sublimation" for many unrestful women. Another strange phenomenon is, that where a little one is adopted as a companion for the only child who frequently leads such a lonely life, the newcomer is soon loved as well as the real son or daughter. Others have engaged in this work. The Spence Alumnæ Society has done so for a long time, and thereby contributed to the rescuing of numerous infants and given happiness to many families. This work thrives best in small units, as does all remedial aid for children. It can be operated all over the country, and, if so, there would soon be few homeless children and childless homes.

The Illegitimate Child

What is to become of the illegitimate child? Is one way better than another in dealing with this difficult question? The extent of the problem varies in different countries and districts. Infants born out of wedlock reach from three to twelve per cent. of all births in civilized countries. There is a yearly average of 32,000 illegitimate births among the white population of the United States. They do not differ much, if any, from other infants except

THE ADOPTION OF CHILDREN 181

that they present a higher death-rate. This is because of lack of proper care, which the deserted mothers are not able to give. In many cases these babies are unusually well formed and attractive.

Most agencies and institutions handling these cases recommend that the mother keep the baby on the ground that her character will be stabilized by love for her child. While this is doubtless true in some cases, I believe, under present social conditions, it is wiser as a rule to separate them and have the child adopted into a good family if marriage is out of the question. My reasons for this are reached after wide experience and observation. In the first place, the child, who is the only innocent party in the whole transaction, should have the primary consideration. To be brought up in a precarious manner by the hard struggles of an unmarried mother, without normal home life, and with the stigma of illegitimacy hanging over its head, is not a happy outlook. The mother herself cannot escape the cruel implication of the scarlet letter. This will all be avoided by having the woman face her trouble away from home, and after nursing her baby long enough to give it a good start, have it adopted into some family able to give protection and

182 HEREDITY AND CHILD CULTURE

training as well as love and thus open the door of future opportunity. Outside of a few intimates, the world can thus be kept in ignorance of the girl's misfortune. I have rarely seen any of these young women who could be considered bad. They are rather ignorant and unsophisticated, and give for love what many better placed women give for position or fortune. There is no connection between this class of women and prostitutes, who usually cannot have children if they would. Thus both woman and child should not be punished but protected, and directed to the wisest outcome of their trouble.

Miss Plows-Day, one of the founders of the National Adoption Society of England, as a result of close personal experience derived from more than twenty years of rescue work among all kinds of fallen women in London, has concluded that if the child is taken entirely out of the unfortunate conditions under which it was born by being properly adopted, it has the very best, if not the only chance for future happiness and health of soul, mind and body. She has recognized the inaccuracy of the argument that a girl who keeps her illegitimate child is less apt to fall again than if she was helped back, as far as possible, to her former

THE ADOPTION OF CHILDREN 183

social and economic position. The contrary has been her experience. While during the child's earliest years it may appear to help steady the mother to let her keep her child, the strained relations will sooner or later have a bad effect upon both child and mother. The mother should thus be taught the desirability of renunciation, and inspired to be willing to sacrifice her claim of motherhood for the benefit of her child.

For women who are in good circumstances the problem is not so difficult. In a few instances it has been arranged that an unmarried mother shall adopt her own baby with our nursery as intermediary. Thus is offered a happy solution of a tragic problem.

Norway has taken a most advanced stand in connection with the legal status of the child born out of wedlock—which is the same in relation to the father as to the mother. Efforts are made to establish the paternity of the child as far as the state can accomplish this. The right of the child overrides the right of the mother in case she wishes to keep this a secret. As a result, 40 per cent. of the illegitimate children in Norway receive support from their fathers. In all these cases paternity had to be established if it was not willingly acknowledged.

184 HEREDITY AND CHILD CULTURE

Until other countries are willing to give a fairer deal to the illegitimate child and better aid to the unmarried mother, adoption of the child into good families is the best solution of the problem in a great majority of cases.

CHAPTER XVI

THE PROLONGATION OF HUMAN LIFE THROUGH CHILD CULTURE

CAN human life be much prolonged? If possible, is such a result desirable? A mere continuation of life, without vigour or productive power, does not present an attractive outlook. Simply to drag out a vegetative existence usually means unhappiness to the individual and too often a burden on society; yet one cannot help feeling that many human lives are too short. Just as the individual learns how to live and begins to accumulate a valuable experience that may be of service to the world, death cuts short the career.

There may be almost unlimited possibilities in the future development of the human race if the span of life can only be lengthened. There is no physiological basis for the three score years and ten that so long have been considered as the satisfactory limit of human life. Naturalists tell us that the length of life in the

185

186 HEREDITY AND CHILD CULTURE

lower animals averages five times the period of the growth of their bones. By analogy, this would mean that the human animal should live to be a hundred.

I believe we may build up a future generation that can reach the century mark if only the developing period can be more carefully cultured. The roots of most degenerative conditions, and many of the infections, have their inception in the early years. Thus, by more carefully nurturing this period we may make the proper start for a long and vigorous existence.

Life may be divided into three spans,—first, that of development ; second, a longer or shorter period of physical stand-still ; and finally a short one of degeneration and decline,—corresponding to childhood, middle age and old age. Each period requires special management, but a right start is the most important of all. I have elsewhere considered the needs of these separate periods and shown how a prolonging of each depends largely upon the proper handling of the previous one.[1] Of late most health work has been devoted to the early years, with the result of a great saving of infant and child life. The expectation of life at birth is

[1] *Health First : The Fine Art of Living*—Century Co.

THE PROLONGATION OF HUMAN LIFE 187

now about ten years greater than it was thirty years ago. This must eventually result in a general prolongation of human life, although it has not yet had time to accomplish such a result.

In various ways, the first and last years of life may be among the most fruitful; if properly envisaged they are likewise the most interesting. At the beginning, the strong foundations for a sound, vigorous existence may be laid. When this is done, the vigour will continue in a long and productive manner. Thus the ending may not be clouded, but rather be full of wise experience, kindly outlook and mellowed vision.

History gives numerous instances where highly productive work was accomplished during advanced years. Dorland calls attention to many of these cases.[1] Verdi was in his eightieth year when he composed " Falstaff "; Oliver Wendell Holmes at seventy-nine published " Over the Tea Cups "; Victor Hugo was eighty when he wrote " Torquemada "; Humbolt was in his ninetieth year when he completed his remarkable work " Kosmos "; Ranke began his world history when he was eighty and finished twelve volumes before his death at ninety-four; Bancroft did not complete his

[1] *The Age of Mental Virility*—Century Co.

188   HEREDITY AND CHILD CULTURE

history until the age of eighty-two ; Browning wrote " Asolando " when he was seventy-six.

The most recent example of productivity at great age is shown by Dr. Stephen Smith who was my preceptor and with whom I lived for two years at the beginning of my professional career. Dr. Smith is now in his hundredth year and at the recent fiftieth aniversary of the American Public Health Association, which he founded, he made a long address on health matters and is now engaged in writing a book. He recently told me that he believes others can reach the same ripened and constructive maturity by hygienic living.

If we can have a good heredity and favourable environment during the early years, there is no doubt that health and vigour may be continued much longer than have usually been attained. The evolution of the human body has been pretty fully accomplished ; Professor Conklin says that for at least one hundred centuries there has been no notable progress in this respect. In stature and skull size we do not appear much better than the Cro-Magnons.

What is left for us is to conserve and improve the mental and spiritual acquirements of the race, based on the physical structure we have inherited from the ages. This means that

THE PROLONGATION OF HUMAN LIFE 189

our years must be carefully husbanded and our productive life, if possible, extended. If we would try for a potent, prolonged and serene old age, we must start early in life,—with the child.

This last chapter, therefore, ends as did the first,—CONCENTRATE ON THE CHILD!

INDEX

Addams, Jane, 152
Adolescence, 92
Adoption of children, 173
— ways and means offered for, 177
Age, the pre-school, 66
— of marriage, 33-39
Alice Chapin adoption nursery, 179
American Child Hygiene Association, 153
— Medical Association, 61
—Public Health Association, 188
Ancestral inheritance, Dalton's Law of, 18-19
Ancient Roman laws for care of dependent children, 174-175
Ants and bees, organization in life of, 24
Aristotle, 35
Athletics, 91
Average weekly gain in infants, 56

Baker, Dr. Josephine, 81
Bancroft, 187
Barbarism in children, 110
Barnes, Prof., 109
Bees and ants, organization in life of, 24
Beginning of life, 43
Biological heredity, 21
— regulation of, 52
— birth mortality and, 46
Birth weight, 53
Brain development, 5
— of the infant, 98-99
Brain, growth and evolution of, 58
Brain structure and functions, 96-97
Breeding, selective, 32
Brooks, Phillips, 171
Brosnan, John Francis, 174
Browning, 188

Calories as measures of food value, 134
Charity organization Society, 63
Chicago High Schools, questionaire in, 103
Child as a creator of affection, the, 142
— importance of the, 3
— the dependent, 149

— health organizations, 76
— the illegitimate, 180
— culture, prolongation of human life through, 185
Child's place in evolution, the, 144
Childhood, development during, 67
Children, adoption of, 172
— undernourished, 136
Children's Village, 29
Communistic philosophers, flaws in reasoning of, 148
Comparative growth of boys and girls in height, 73
Complexes, 120-122
Conception, development of life after, 44
— principles of, 43
Conklin Prof. Edwin Grant, 15, 20, 26, 38, 174, 188
Conn, Prof. Herbert William, 20, 21, 26
Conscience, development of, 23
Conservation as preparatory foundation for improving social structure, 7
Conserving infant life, 61
Contagion among institution children, 154-155
Correct posture, 87
Cows' Milk, care in collection and distribution of, 131
Crum, Mr. F. S., 61
Darwin, 11, 12
Darwin, Major Leonard, 32
Defective hygiene in child institutions , 156
— vision in rural school children, 86
Defectives, propagation of, 38
— suggestions for curbing, 40
Delinquency, childhood traits and, 113
Dentition, process of, 60
Dependent children, public system for care of in various states, 151
Developing period, the, 52
Devine, Prof. E. P., 166-167
Diet for nursing mother, 130

INDEX

191

Divorce, one of the greatest evils of, 147

Doncaster, Prof., 25

Dorland, 187

Eating slowly, value and importance of, 131

Education, 101
— and instruction, 104
— the senses in, 102

Educational work in Speedwell System, 161

Embryo, development of, 44

Emerson, Dr. Wm. R. P., 136, 137, 138

Endocrine glands, importance of, 112

England, care of dependent children in, 178

Environment in life, heredity and, 3
— or heredity, importance contrasted, 10

European laws on care of dependent children, 175

Evolution, development of conscience in, 23
— forces producing, 11
— and growth of brain, 58
— language in 22
— writing in, 23
— moral sense and, 23

Family, the, 140

Farmers' Bulletin No. 808 of the United States Government, 133

Fear to be avoided, 122

Federal Children's Bureau, 61, 63, 67

Ferguson, 30

Fiske, John, 4, 140

Folks, Homer, 151

Food principles, 125

Forces producing evolution, 11

Franklin, Benj., 35

Freud, 120

Galton's law of ancestral inheritance, 18-19

Girl's, higher education for, 105-106

Growth during infancy, 52

Hall, Prof. G. Stanley, 107

Harris, Dr. Elisha, 150

Height, comparative growth of boys and girls in, 73-74

Heredity, Biological, regulation of, 52
— biological and social, 21
— views of biologists on, 11

— or environment, discussion of relative importance of, 10
— and environment as controlling factors in life, 3

Higher education for girls, 105-106

Holmes, Dr., 46, 51

Holmes, Oliver Wendell, 187

Hrdlicka, Dr. Ales, 114

Hugo, Victor, 187

Humbolt, 187

Hygiene in child institutions, defective, 156

Illegitimate children, Norway's stand on legal status of, 183

Illegitimate child, the, 180

Imitation and suggestion in mental development, 99

Importance of the child, the, 3
— of proper nutrition, the, 124

Infancy, growth during, 52
— period of, 4

Infant mortality among foundlings in institutions, 158

Infection among institution children, 154-155
— in childhood, 69

Inheritance, organic, 10
— social, 20
— social and organic, 28
— Galton's law of ancestral, 18-19

Instincts, origin and function of, 24

Instruction and education, 104

International Conference for Child Welfare, 164
— Conference of Red Cross Societies, 156

Iowa school children, conclusions resulting from study of, 76
— study of 40,000 children in, 68

Lamarck, 11

Language, place of in evolution, 21

Length and structural characteristics of infants at birth, 55-56

Life, beginning of, 43
— three spans of, 186

Loeb, Miss, 169

Lombroso, 110-111

Lying as a child fault, 109

Malnutrition in school children, 86
— its effect and cure, 136-137

192 INDEX

Marriage, age of, 34-36
"Maternal impression" bugbear disproved, 50
Maternity, preparations for, 48
— mental preparations for, 50
Mating, discussions of conditions of, 36
Mendel, Gregor, 15
Mendelism, 15
Mental Culture, 96
Mercier, Dr. Charles, 43
Milk as a food, 127-131
Moral Culture, 109
— sense and evolution, 23
Mortality and birth, 46
Motherhood, schools of, 146
Musculature in infancy, 59

Nerve culture, 119
Neurotics, 119-120
New York Board of Health, 72
— City, reduction of infant mortality, in, 61
— Juvenile Asylum, 114
Newman, Sir George, 6, 33
Norway's stand on legal status of illegitimate children, 183
Nursemaids, mistake of employing ignorant, 146
Nursing mother, Diet for, 130
Nutrition, importance of proper, 124

Organic inheritance, 10
— and social inheritance, 28
Organization in life of bees and ants, 24
Osborn, Prof. Henry Fairfield, 16
Osborne, Thomas Mott, 168

Paton, Professor Stewart, 22
Pearson, 18
Period, the developing, 52
— of infancy, 4
Play, teaching children to, 115
Plows-Day, Miss, 182
Precocious children, 99
Pre-natal care, 46
Pre-school age, the, 66
Prolongation of human life through child culture, 185.
Public Systems for the care of dependent children in various states, 151

Ranke, 187
Redfield, Casper L., 35-36
Religious training, 116
Royal Sanitary Institue of Great Britain, tabulated report of, 90
Rural schools, 86

School child, the, 73
— equipment, 88
Selective breeding, 32
Selfishness, elimination of, 115
Senses in education, 102
Sex education of children, 111
Sexual selection, advisabiltty of, 33
Smith, Dr. Stephen, 188
Sobel, Dr., 72
Social Heredity, 21
— inheritance and organic inheritance, 28
— inheritance, 20
Spaulding, Dr., 121
Speedwell System, the, 154n, 159-168.
Spence Alumnae Society, 180
Spinal column in infancy, 59
State Board of Charities of New York, Report of, 153
Stoddard, Lathrop, 26
Structural development of the infant, 57
Suggestion in mental development, imitation and, 99
System, the Speedwell, 154n, 159-168

Teeth in childhood, care of, 71
Thinking, the value of correct, 103
Traffic in Babies, 154n

Units in the Speedwell System, 159-168

Vacations in schools, 106
Verdi, 187
Vitamines, 125-127

Weight of infants at birth, 52
— weekly average gain of, 54
— increase of at 5 to 6 months, 55
— relation of to development, 75
Weismann, Doctrine of, 13
Weismann, 25, 36
Weismann's distinction between hereditary forces and their visible expressions, 17
Widows' Pension Law, 169
Wood, Dr. Thomas D., 76, 86-87
Writing as a factor in evolution, 22